Immigrant Networks and Social Capital

Immigration & Society series

Carl L. Bankston III, *Immigrant Networks and Social Capital*

Thomas Faist, Margit Fauser, & Eveline Reisenauer, *Transnational Migration*

Christian Joppke, *Citizenship and Immigration*

Grace Kao, Elizabeth Vaquera, & Kimberly Goyette, *Education and Immigration*

Nazli Kibria, Cara Bowman, & Megan O'Leary, *Race and Immigration*

Peter Kivisto, *Religion and Immigration*

Ronald L. Mize & Grace Peña Delgado, *Latino Immigrants in the United States*

Philip Q. Yang, *Asian Immigration to the United States*

Immigrant Networks and Social Capital

Carl L. Bankston III

polity

First published in 2014 by Polity Press

Polity Press
65 Bridge Street
Cambridge CB2 1UR, UK

Polity Press
350 Main Street
Malden, MA 02148, USA

ISBN-13: 978-0-7456-6236-7
ISBN-13: 978-0-7456-6237-4(pb)

A catalogue record for this book is available from the British Library.

Typeset in 11 on 13 pt Sabon by
Servis Filmsetting Ltd, Stockport, Cheshire
Printed and bound in Great Britain by Clays Ltd, St Ives Plc

The publisher has used its best endeavours to ensure that the URLs for external websites referred to in this book are correct and active at the time of going to press. However, the publisher has no responsibility for the websites and can make no guarantee that a site will remain live or that the content is or will remain appropriate.

Every effort has been made to trace all copyright holders, but if any have been inadvertently overlooked the publisher will be pleased to include any necessary credits in any subsequent reprint or edition.

For further information on Polity, visit our website: www.politybooks.com

Contents

Introduction:
Beyond Individual Migration

The Limitations of Individual-Level Approaches

Social capital accounts of immigration using social networks are essentially ways of thinking about the issue of immigration in terms of how people in immigrant groups are connected to each other. Group-level approaches can move us beyond thinking about immigration in terms of individual immigrant characteristics, a dominant tendency in early immigration research that continues to exercise some influence today. The historically influential assimilationist perspective, in particular, tended to take an individual-level approach to immigration and immigrant adaptation (see the work of Robert Park, 1928; Irving Child, 1943; and Milton Gordon, 1964).

The idea that adaptation consists of individuals gradually becoming part of a host society continues to be part of the study of migration. An individual-level assimilation approach leaves many questions unanswered. Why do different groups occupy different places in the host country economy from the time of their arrival? Why do group members often tend to continue to be associated with those places even after many of their individual members have been culturally or structurally assimilated? Why are some groups economically successful even though in some respects they may remain culturally distinctive?

One way to answer this question might be to concentrate on pre-migration characteristics, rather than on post-migration developments such as assimilation. Members of different immigrant groups leave their countries with different resources, and they pass those resources on to their children. Along these lines, human capital views emphasize resources such as education, skills, or familiarity with the host country brought from the country of origin. Given the fact that receiving countries often admit immigrants who possess valued skills and education, human capital unquestionably plays a part in determining who will migrate and where they will end up in the host country's socioeconomic system. The distinction between legally admitted immigrants and entrants without documents itself may be regarded as a human capital issue. Legal status is an asset possessed by individual immigrants and it can be a basis for acquiring more skills and education (Pan, 2012). Moreover, the different types of human capital that members of different immigrant groups tend to possess can play a large part in shaping the structure of ethnic stratification, as well as the socioeconomic locations of individual immigrants. Experience in unskilled or semi-skilled blue-collar work can channel members of some groups into occupations such as construction, while professional credentials direct others elsewhere. Thus, the disproportionate representation of Mexicans and Central Americans in construction and of South Asians in medical occupations can be treated as a matter of human capital slotting individual members of groups into an existing system of labor demand.

While human capital approaches are useful because they look at migration in terms of emigration as well as immigration, these approaches tend to consider only individual skills or credentials, and even when individuals have these, the skills or credentials alone do not determine destinies. Migration itself, however, cannot be reduced to individual characteristics alone. Chain migration, the tendency of migrants to follow their kin and home country associates to a new land, means that from the very beginning migration is a profoundly social process, based on social connections. In order to explain why people migrate and how pre-migration characteristics and post-migration destinies are linked together, we need to look at the whole process of migration and immigrant adaptation as a function of social patterns. In this book, I consider the ideas of immigrant networks and social capital as ways of thinking about the social connections that move people from one place to another and shape their lives as dwellers in a new land.

Organization of the Book

The goal of this book is to look at how patterns of social connections come into existence and at how those patterns of connections account for processes of migration and immigrant outcomes. To do this, the book intends to: (1) clearly define social networks and social capital, (2) offer a broad theoretical discussion of the main issues relating to social networks and social capital among immigrants, and (3) illustrate how network and social capital approaches can account for immigration and variation among immigrant groups.

Chapter 1 begins with a general look at social network approaches to immigration. I provide a theoretical introduction to the idea of networks in immigration by describing how networks may be viewed either as communities or as patterns of communication. We typically think of immigrant networks as located within ethnic neighborhoods, although a spatial community may take other forms. This is the version of immigrant networks most often presented in social capital approaches (as in Zhou and Bankston, 1998; 2000). Networks may also be considered as patterns in the flow of communications, though. From the communication perspective, the flow of information defines the connections among people (Kao, 2004). Accounts of network-based international migration and secondary migration tend to emphasize lines of communication across geographic space (as in Light, 2006). Both factual information (such as the availability of jobs, housing, or educational opportunities) and cultural information (such as norms and values, judgments of individuals and groups, and perceptions of life possibilities) move along communication lines. I discuss the ways in which these two ways of thinking about networks, as spatial communities and as patterns of communication, are interrelated.

Then I discuss networks as sets of connections within and

across group boundaries in modern pluralistic societies. Social networks connect individuals to other individuals in theoretically identifiable arrangements, either in communities or through lines of communication. However, networks also connect people within groups and they link people across groups. Therefore, we can think of networks as based on links among individuals, as groups that provide foundations for linkages among people, or as ways in which groups, as bounded sets of individuals, are linked to each other. I discuss how connections within and across network boundaries may help us understand issues such as ethnic stratification and ethnic specialization.

At the end of Chapter 1, I set the stage for moving on to a theoretical consideration of social capital by looking at networks as providing bridging ties and bonding ties. This contrast follows logically from the discussion of individuals and groups in the previous subsection and it raises the crucial point for social capital: what are the consequences of social bonds? This section discusses the idea that social ties can be seen as bringing resources or information to groups or individuals (bridges) or as creating strong ties of support and control (bonds).

Following the identification of the main theoretical issues relating to networks, with special reference to immigrants, Chapter 2 discusses primary issues involved in the concept of social capital. I begin by briefly discussing how researchers and theorists have come to conceive of social relations as assets for advancement on the analogy of financial capital. I mention some of the questions about this analogy, and I point out that social capital theory should be employed heuristically and with caution in the study of immigration. Then I look at the ways in which social relations, particularly network ties, may produce outcomes for members of social groups, particularly immigrant groups.

I look at social capital considered as solidarity and social capital considered as norms, and I follow this by examining how ties among people can create resources by enabling people to cooperate in order to achieve collective and individual ends or by constraining people to direct their actions. I consider social resources as matters of patterns of individual interactions and as more or less formal organizations, and I discuss how patterns of interactions and formal organizations are interrelated.

I move on to an examination of what kinds of "investments" social capital can be directed toward. I identify three types of investments that are especially important for immigrants. In the most basic sense, social relations can be considered as "capital" because they create financial assets, most notably by encouraging trust that can be translated into credit. One of the most common topics in the social capital literature is how networks can produce human capital, usually through providing support and control leading to educational advancement among young people. As a final part of this section of the chapter, I consider how immigrant networks can offer opportunities in the broader sense, through the information and mutual assistance that can put immigrants in touch with jobs and housing.

The theoretical introduction to social capital in immigration ends by examining the major shortcomings and problems of the concept of social capital. Following the question of where social capital is invested, I raise the question of whether network ties among members of immigrant groups serve to promote psychological adaptation or promote upward mobility. Connected to this, I consider the issue of "negative social capital." If connections among people can constitute assets, then, logically, they may also constitute liabilities. But how can "capital" be a liability? I suggest that this problem indicates that we should approach social capital accounts of immigrant adaptation as based on an imperfect metaphor and that this should be continually kept in mind.

Insofar as social capital is similar to financial capital, the former, like the latter, may not be an unqualified good for all parties at all times. Social capital is, like financial capital, often deeply involved in competition and conflict among different parts of a society. Since social capital is shared within groups in competition with outsiders for scarce resources, it is a bit like insider trading, and group members may benefit from the exclusion of outsiders. The "balkanization" problem is related to this. High levels of cohesion within groups may lead to distrust and limited interaction across groups.

In Chapter 3, I move from theoretical issues regarding networks and social capital to discussing how these concepts may account for immigration and immigrant adaptation. I begin this chapter with a general overview of how social networks bring immigrants to a host country in social, political, and economic conditions within and across national boundaries. I use as my primary examples four major groups: Mexicans, Koreans, Vietnamese, and Filipinos. I use these immigrant groups as reference points for several reasons. First, each of them illustrates some of the major issues concerning how immigrant networks affect the social resources of groups. Second, all of these are major immigrant categories. About three-quarters of immigration to the United States since the early 1970s has consistently come from Latin America and Asia. Mexicans make up by far the largest Latin American category and the other three are all among the largest national-origin groups from Asia. Third, I have done some research and writing on all four of these and therefore have some knowledge and background understanding of their immigration. My goal, however, is not to give histories of these specific national-origin categories of immigrants but to use these examples as cases to examine how social networks function as resources for immigrants and immigrant groups in general.

I begin with discussing how social networks are related to contexts of exit and contexts of reception, illustrating this with the four groups. I then link the topics of contexts of exit and reception to that of the global economy, looking at economic supply in countries of origin, demand for labor in the United States, and how interpersonal networks across nations fill possibilities created by the global economy, again using those four groups as examples.

Chapter 4 examines family ties. It describes the role of family in bringing immigrants into the United States and in determining their responses to the new environment, while also identifying how family networks are reshaped by immigration. Again, I make this examination of family ties within immigrant groups by brief discussions of selected immigrant groups. Chapter 5 moves from families to larger social groups. After examining family connections and their consequences, I broaden the consideration of networks and the social resources they can produce by looking

6

at the kinds of communities that ethnic groups may form. I look at the enclave, defined as a relatively self-contained social and economic geographic unit, and the neighborhood, a place where members of an ethnic group reside, as well as at immigrant communities that are not clearly defined by geography. I use these ideas about different types of communities to look at how networks beyond kin may lead to varying consequences for groups, or produce social capitals.

In Chapter 6, I look at the work of formal institutions in immigrant communities and describe how formal institutions may fit into the kinds of communities described in Chapter 5. Scott Feld's concept of the "network focus" lies at the core of this chapter, which argues that formal institutions or associations are best seen as focal points that coordinate network relations. This chapter looks at consequences for immigrants of relatively weak organizations and argues that "strong" formal institutions tend to consist of networks that are internally differentiated and have "bottom-up" direction and control from group members. I argue that religion often provides particularly effective formal organizations for immigrant groups. Organizations, however, do not exist in isolation and interconnections among organizations, as among individuals, can provide immigrants with important assets. At the end of the chapter, I discuss an often overlooked aspect of immigrant organizations: their capacity to provide symbolic representations of group identity, often maintaining network ties and cooperation among people in immigrant groups frequently thought of as highly assimilated.

The final two chapters consider how social ties affect immigrant adaptation in two key areas: employment and education. In looking at how social ties affect employment, I differentiate between ethnic jobs, in which ethnicity is associated with a particular niche or type of work, and ethnic economies, in which ethnicity becomes the basis of economic interaction among group members, most notably through entrepreneurship. The chapter illustrates the idea of ethnic jobs mainly through reference to the largest immigrant nationalities in the United States: Mexicans and those from elsewhere in Latin America, who constitute a substantial portion of the nation's working class. Following the discussion of ethnic jobs, I examine how networks and social resources can shape economic relations among immigrant groups and among ethnic and racial groups within the United States. I start this by examining the phenomenon of Korean employers and Mexican workers. From this, I move on to considering Korean entrepreneurs as examples of the "middleman minority," focusing on the network and social capital issues raised earlier in the book. A third section of Chapter 7 extends these ideas by examining how concentrations in ethnic economies are related to ethnic jobs. The last part of the chapter turns to ethnic professions, pointing that while networks channel some immigrant groups into working-class jobs, they direct others toward professional concentrations.

Chapter 8 discusses how social ties may be related to intergenerational mobility through the education of young immigrants and children of immigrants. Although we usually think of immigrant network connections as compensatory, in the sense that they make possible socioeconomic mobility for those at the margins of the American economy, we can also see immigrant network connections as complementary, in the sense that links to other group members can also enhance the ability of professional immigrants to pass high levels of human capital on to their children. The chapter describes how network constraints may be positively or negatively related to educational achievement and attainment. The chapter then connects the role of social ties in economic adaptation to educational adaptation by discussing how cooperative economic relations and attitudes among those in one generation may provide a base for upward mobility in a succeeding generation. Pursuing the idea of complementary social capital, I consider situations in which immigrant networks promote school performance among professional immigrants and even among members of immigrant groups who appear to have assimilated in many respects. I end with the controversial idea of "generational decline," suggesting that "decline" can mean different things for descendants of different immigrant groups, ranging from possible assimilation into alienated, oppositional segments of American society to a simple leveling-off of an initial high rate of upward mobility. In this chapter, I discuss one of the seldom recognized ironies of educational achievement through ethnic solidarity: successful social networks among immigrant groups in the United States may ultimately lead to their own loosening and even dissolution as group social capital is transformed into individual human capital across generations.

The conclusion summarizes the similarities and differences in the ways that social networks function among different immigrant groups. Based on this summary, I suggest that ideas of social networks and social capital theory can be integrated with traditional push–pull accounts of immigration by considering the ways in which international connections come into existence. These connections, together with economic trends within nations, shape interpersonal relations within and across nations. Family and community networks, as well as formal organizations, take their forms from these interpersonal relations. In turn, ethnic networks mobilize and support individuals for specific types of activities in American society. I discuss how networks and social capital can not only help us understand contemporary immigration, but also provide ways of thinking about broader theoretical questions in the social sciences, such as how structure and agency work together and how individuals fit into groups.

1

Social Networks in Immigration

The questions of how individual people are connected to each other, what these connections enable them to do, and how these connections limit what they can do are some of the oldest in the discipline of sociology. The issues of how people are bound together and how their ties serve or diminish their collective and individual efficacy continue to be central to social theory today. Network theory is a way to examine those ties as patterns of links among people. To prepare to look at how networks may be considered as resources for immigrants, this chapter will provide a general discussion of network concepts, as these relate to immigration.

Network Communities and Communication

The word "community" may be one of the most over-used and contentious terms in the social sciences (Brint, 2001). In discussing the use of the word as it relates to immigration research, Wierzbicki (2004) has suggested that it has three main senses. One of these refers to the community as a physical location, a sense that has been common within community studies. Many of the immigrant communities that the present book will consider have a grounding in physical location. For example, the set of social ties that comprise the Vietnamese community discussed by Zhou and Bankston (1998) takes shape within a physical location that enables group members to have and maintain contacts. The organizations that can serve as focal points for network ties among people often do so by bringing people into the same geographical space for at least temporary periods. Thus, although we can think of a place as some sort of "community" merely because people live in it, which is what Wierzbicki means in speaking of it in this first sense, when we think about a community as a network, the physical location is important only because it establishes relationships among the people in it. In this sense, a physical community conceived of as a network can be defined as a set of social ties that can be located on a map. Even geographically extended networks can be thought of as communities in space in this sense. One could, for example, place on a map the relationships among Asian Indian motel owners along interstate highways, and conceive of this as a spatial community, if one stretched out across some very wide spaces (see Dhingra, 2010; 2012).

A second sense of the word "community," Wierzbicki points out, is a group of people who have something in common, without necessarily knowing each other, such as "the Republican community" or "the African American community." This is the loosest sense of the word. It can, however, have some relationship to the idea of a network as a community. Homophily, or the tendency of people to form social connections on the basis of common interests, backgrounds, and identities, can make social categories bases for interpersonal associations. Alternatively, repeated transactions can produce and maintain categorical identities for groups. Thus, Charles Tilly (1978) described a set of people who are members of both a social category and a social network as a "catnet."

Community as network is a third sense of the word (Wierzbicki, 2004). Along these lines, Barry Wellman (1999) argues that the network is the contemporary answer to the question of what constitutes a community in a society in which social relations can no longer be looked at solely in terms of place. A network links people in an identifiable set of relationships. These relationships have an internal organization. This organization has the property of density: when all those within it have relationships with each other, this is high density. When most of the people in the network are connected to others indirectly, through shared associations, this is low density. It has the property of strength or weakness of ties. While there is some debate about just what a strong or weak tie might be, in general we can take this to refer to the intensity of relationships. We have strong ties with our family members and close friends and relatively weaker ties with mere co-workers or occasional associates. A network characterized by strong ties is one in which most people maintain close relationships with each other. Frequency of contact is a property often confused with strength of ties because people often have frequent contacts with their close associates and because repeated contacts can promote strong ties. Nan Lin (1999) has observed that individuals possess both strong and weak ties, and that combining these may enable them to obtain the greatest range of resources.

In addition to internal organization, networks can differ in their linkages with the world outside of them and in size. The network may be relatively closed or open. A closed network is one in which most social relationships in a community are with other members of the community. An open network is one in which people have many links to people outside the community. Networks can, finally, be large or small, containing many members or comparatively few.

Because I am concerned primarily with immigrant groups, rather than with individuals, in this discussion and in these figures, I am looking at what Wellman (1999) calls whole networks, rather than at networks as personal communities, understood as the ties that link a given individual to others.

In whole networks considered as relational structures, the central focus is on the participants as points of connection. If we map out a set of network contacts, we can represent the structure of the network community in terms of any of its properties. For example, a small Cambodian social network in Houston can be represented by drawing thick lines between all those who have especially strong ties with each other, somewhat thinner lines to represent those linked together by bonds of close association (such as friend-ship), and broken lines to represent more casual acquaintances. In the idealized map in Figure 1.1, for example, all of the individuals have social contacts, but those in the center (X_1 through X_5) are all strongly connected as members of a family. Here, X_1 and X_2 can represent parents and the others in the center children. X_6 through X_9 are non-family Cambodians, all linked to family members by ties of close association. The only ties to people who are not Cambodians (Y_1 and Y_2) are through non-family members of the ethnic group. A similar kind of map might represent frequency of contacts among members of this Cambodian community, with the thickness and continuity of the lines representing numbers of contacts in a period of time, rather than intensity of relationship. The design resulting from either could yield an approximation of how closed or open that community is, through the number and type of lines going outside the community, and an approximation of its size. It would also give an idea of how legitimate it would be to speak of a Cambodian community in Houston, rather than simply individuals of Cambodian ancestry settled there. If the lines were not concentrated among people of Cambodian ethnicity (again, the role of community as commonality of identity), then

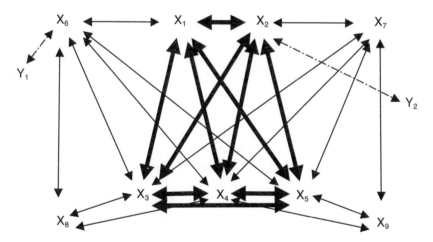

Figure 1.1   Networks as Structures of Relations: Strong and Weak Ties among Individuals

Notes: ◄——► = Family tie;   ◄——► = Close association;
◄ —·—·► = Casual acquaintance.
X = Cambodian; Y = Non-Cambodian.

13

one could argue that Houston really has no Cambodian community, in the sense of Tilly's "catnet," even though it may have many individuals of Cambodian ancestry and identification. This idealized version shows a closed ethnically based network, since only two Cambodians have ties to non-Cambodians.

In the social networks literature, the concepts of network closure and density are related to the idea of transitivity, which exists to the extent that the individuals to whom two people are connected are also connected to each other (Flynn et al., 2010). Figure 1.1 shows complete transitivity among all Cambodians, since each individual in this categorically defined network is connected to all others. Multiplexity, a similar property, refers to the degree to which two individuals are tied to each other in different ways (Skoretz and Agneesens, 2007); for example, if two individuals are friends, neighbors, and co-workers. Within networks, the centrality of individuals deals with how key they are to connecting others. While technical approaches to network analysis define and measure centrality in a number of ways (see del Pozo et al., 2011), for simplicity we can consider centrality as the extent to which an individual is central in connecting other individuals.

Networks may be relatively egalitarian in relations among actors or they may involve hierarchies of power, prestige, and access to resources. Some authors have argued that multi-layering and hierarchy can promote the abilities of networks to coordinate activities among members and distribute information efficiently (David-Barrett and Dunbar, 2012). Figure 1.2 shows a simple network structured by unequal relations between a workplace supervisor and the workers, and equal relations among workers, where X = Cambodian.

This idea of lines among points suggests that we can look at networks in terms of what flows along those lines, or of what kinds of communication move through social connections. From this perspective, the focus in looking at the network would be on considering how the information about opportunities, resources, or such immaterial matters as norms and values can be conveyed through structures of relations. The idealized and simplified version presented in Figure 1.3 illustrates how a network can

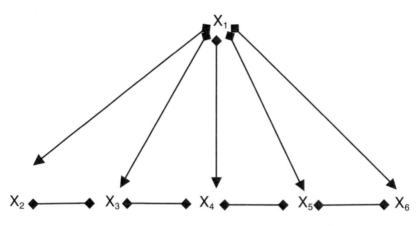

Figure 1.2   Inequality in a Network Structure

Notes: ◆——▶ = Supervisor–worker relationship;
◆——◆ = Co-worker relationship.

provide channels for communication of information about two resources: employment and housing. Here, members of the group are assumed to receive both kinds of information from those outside the group, with communications about housing entering the group as a result of the link between non-Cambodian Y_1 and Cambodian X_3 and communications about employment entering along the link between Y_2 and X_2. (Although idealized, this diagram is based on the real-world case of the Lao community discussed in Chapter 6.)

There is a tendency in theorizing about networks, especially in thinking about networks as sources of more or less constructive social action, to emphasize the structural properties of sets of social relations. Thus, although James Coleman (1988; 1990) recognizes that networks serve as information channels, he tends to treat the functioning of social ties as a matter of properties such as network closure. Highly transitive, multiplex networks, moreover, can intensify the sharing of information and normative orientations, while also limiting the flow of new information inward. Individuals who occupy positions of centrality can facilitate communication among others, while hierarchical structuring

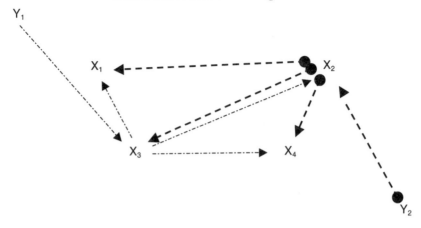

Figure 1.3 Network as Communication Channels

Notes: ● – – ➤ = Employment information;
·—·—·➤ = Housing information.
X = Cambodian; Y = Non-Cambodian.

can increase communicative efficiency. As I will attempt to demonstrate in the following pages, though, one of the reasons that sets of connections among people provide varying outcomes for different groups of people is that those connections contain different sorts of information. In addition to the geometric arrangement of contacts among people, one needs to consider what can be conveyed through those contacts. Culture, especially as expectations and norms, can be considered part of the available information. If members of an immigrant group have an expectation of upward mobility for themselves or their children, for example, close ties among members of the group that reinforce this expectation can contribute to realizing it. If group experiences have produced a general expectation that there is little possibility of mobility, then the same geometric arrangement of ties can actually limit chances.

More material sorts of information can also be influential. If some group members know of the availability of job or housing opportunities, this knowledge can move along the lines of connection among other members. This means that the kinds of knowledge or norms that can be shared are critical, and the larger setting that determines what kind of information group members can access and share shapes the nature of networks as lines of communication. For example, the concentration of Mexican immigrants in semi-skilled and unskilled labor in specific industries is, at one level, a matter of individuals being channeled by the types of knowledge that move through their ethnic networks and, at another level, a matter of group placement in North American labor market demand, which limits and structures the information about jobs available, as well as expectations.

Networks Within and Across Group Boundaries

Social networks connect individuals to other individuals in theoretically identifiable arrangements. However, networks also connect people within and across these identifiable arrangements. Therefore, we can think of networks based on links among individuals as groups that provide foundations for linkages among sets of people, or as ways in which people are linked to each other across groups that are bounded by ties based on shared identification (such as "catnets").

The idea of networks as linking people across group boundaries has particular application to conceptualizing the phenomenon of ethnic stratification. The term "stratification" inclines us to think about structured inequality as a matter of distinct strata or layers. Applied to immigrant ethnicities, this gives us the image of members of different groups distributed in layers, according to occupational prestige, income, and educational levels.

In briefly describing the structural properties of networks, I mentioned network size, or number of members, as one of the influences on how individuals within groups interact. The relative size of different groups may also influence relations across group boundaries. Peter Blau (1977; Blau et al., 1982; 1984; Blau and Schwartz, 1984), for example, considered group sizes as a key to group interactions, arguing that individuals in smaller groups tend to have more interactions with outsiders, including higher levels of exogamy, than larger groups do. However, the nature and frequency of links across groups are also influenced by other properties, such as closure. Independent of size, a group with a high degree of closure will necessarily have fewer cross-group links than one that is more open. The relatively closed social network, considered as a flow of information, will tend to concentrate communication within a group and bring in only selective information from outside. Clearly, qualities such as size and permeability do not simply influence the lives of individual group members, but also affect how the group as a whole interacts with other groups, and its placement within the social structure conceived as a network of groups.

To make this more concrete, we can think of ethnic-concentration occupations as sets of bounded networks within the job market. In New York, for example, Korean greengrocers generally hire Mexican workers (see chapter 4 in Ness, 2005). Rather than seeing this as a matter of individual Koreans connecting with individual Mexicans, we can see this as one of Koreans occupying positions in small business through their links with other Koreans and of Mexicans occupying positions in manual labor through their links with other Mexicans, with both operating in the larger environment of the American labor market. The high degree of concentration of both of the groups can be at least partially attributed to relatively closed networks that limit the flow of information. There are also, however, points of connection across the boundaries of the immigrant ethnic networks that produce highly constrained interactions.

Thinking of networks as patterns of interactions among identifiable groups leads to an issue regarding the properties of networks that deserves special attention, particularly from the perspective of how networks may or may not serve as assets. This is the issue of bonding versus bridging ties.

Bridges and Bonds in Networks

Network properties such as closure, density, and transitivity affect the flow of information, with access to resources constituting a particular type of information flow. Network properties shape relations across groups and therefore direct the amount and types of information that can flow across groups. The intensity and frequency of connections across groups can be considered a key characteristic of these intergroup relations. These connections across groups, though, may also be related to connections within groups.

Bridging ties are those that link individuals in bounded networks to individuals outside the network boundaries, as in the cases of ties between X_6 and Y_1 and X_2 and Y_2 in Figure 1.1, and between X_3 and Y_1 and X_2 and Y_2 in Figure 1.3. Bonding ties are those that link individuals within bounded networks to each other. Bonding ties are typically associated with high degrees of cohesion, identification, motivation, and control. Bridging ties are typically associated with social diversity, relative anonymity, multiplicity of resources, and personal autonomy. Social networks characterized by a preponderance of bonding ties have much more definite boundaries, while those with many bridging ties tend to be loose and porous.

Many of those who write about social capital will discuss the two types of connections as "bridging social capital" and "bonding social capital." Carefully considered, though, since these are types of links among people, rather than outcomes of links, bridges and bonds should be regarded as network characteristics, which may work as assets. Nevertheless, in social capital research, the bridging–bonding distinction is important because it is associated with how networks function for those inside of them and for interactions across groups. Karlan et al. (2009) found that bonding ties and bridging ties yield different kinds of transfers. Consistent with the idea that bonding ties are rich in trust, Karlan and his co-authors found that bonding ties based on dense networks allow the ready transfer of valuable assets among group members. Bridging ties, on the other hand, yield greater access to information, which entails less risk for the parties involved. One clear implication of this finding is that the value of the two kinds of ties for members of immigrant groups depends on what kinds of assets members of a group can access, how available assets are from outside the group, what kinds of information can be found through connections to outsiders, and how dependent individuals are on the flow of external information.

If, for example, individuals in immigrant or other minority groups can readily obtain bank loans and mortgages, then they will be less reliant on co-ethnics for valuable assets. On the other hand, if their co-ethnics have funds for lending or can collectively raise funds, and group members have difficulty obtaining these from the formal institutions of the host country, then the trust created by bonding ties may be a primary financial asset. When groups can generate relatively few assets of their own, or when finding out about opportunities or resources outside the group is especially important, then social ties that create bridges to the outside can be critical.

A set of people must share bonding ties in order for us to describe the group as a definable network with insiders and outsiders. We can, for example, think of individuals who have connections to many other individuals who are not connected to each other. In that case, each individual has her or his own network, but there is nothing to mark off a common network within a set of people.

The bonding–bridging distinction is closely associated with the distinction between "strong ties" and "weak ties." The latter distinction owes much to Mark Granovetter's classic article (1973) on "the strength of weak ties." Granovetter argued that weak ties offered advantages over strong ties in connecting people to employment opportunities. This was because weaker social relations brought in information from a wider and more distant range of sources. Essentially, he argued that weak ties tended to be bridges, extending individual-level networks outside of their bounded group-level networks.

In the study of immigrant adaptation, one of the key questions concerns whether strong, bonding ties or weak, bridging ties serve immigrants more efficiently. This question should be considered in terms of ends, alternatives, and resources. Control and direction through strong, bonding ties is often considered important in the education of young members of immigrant groups. If one looks at networks from the perspective of maximizing economic opportunities, though, then the relative value of bonding or bridging ties depends on what options are available within an immigrant group and on what options are available from the outside. Wide-ranging links outside one's own group may be of little value if all of those links are with people who have little to offer. The strength or weakness of social ties, similarly, may be of greater or lesser value depending on how those ties serve to increase and distribute resources among those in a network (Ryan, 2011).

These issues of the value of networks and what networks may be used for look at social networks from an explicitly functional perspective. Links among people are assumed to provide them with ways of achieving goals. To consider networks in this way is to look at them as assets; that is, as forms of social capital.

2

Immigration and Social Capital

The discussion of bonding and bridging ties and the related contrast of strong and weak ties in Chapter 1 presents a functional, goal-oriented view of social networks: what kinds of connections among people serve ends for groups and for individuals in groups. In matters of immigration, how do network ties enable people to move from one place to another, to subsist, and to seek out opportunities? What kinds of ties are best for these purposes? How, in other words, can social networks serve as assets for immigrants?

Financial, Human, and Social Resources for Investment

The term "social capital" refers to the idea that relationships among people may be assets that can produce favorable outcomes for those involved in the relationships. "Capital," in its most traditional sense, refers to an economic surplus, which is invested to yield an additional surplus, or profit, rather than consumed. From this traditional use of capital, identified as "financial capital," economists derived the idea of "human capital." For an individual, obtaining training and credentials can result in later increases in income and occupational opportunities. For an organization or social group, producing people with training and credentials can raise shared productivity. Cultivating vocational skills or educational certifications, then, constitutes an investment, and the skills and certifications can be seen as forms of capital.

"Social capital" is a further elaboration of the idea of assets for investment. The pay-off of financial and human capital depends on how people collaborate. A business endeavor by people who cannot cooperate is unlikely to result in a profit, regardless of how well financed it is or how well trained its participants are. The conceptualization of social capital is frequently vague, and the term has been used in such a wide variety of ways that it is often difficult to define precisely (Portes, 1998). Nonetheless, as Portes (1998: 4) observes, "despite these differences [in usage], the consensus is growing that social capital stands for the ability of actors to gain benefits by virtue of membership in social networks or other social structures."

The idea that social relations can enable profitable or constructive action is as old as sociology, but the economist Glenn Loury (1977) popularized the term when he used "social capital" to refer to the resources inherent in family relations and in community organizations for the development of young children. Loury's line of argument has clear implications for the study of immigration, since it calls attention to the part played by social structures such as family relations and community organizations in the processes of migration and adaptation to a new country.

One of the answers to the question of what makes social relations assets (or liabilities) has been normative. When members of a group hold norms and values that encourage constructive cooperation, they can be considered to have a form of social capital. According to Francis Fukuyama (1999: 16), "social capital can be defined simply as a set of informal values or norms shared among members of a group that permit cooperation among them."

The issue of norms and values raises the question of whether cultural characteristics may be considered as assets in themselves. Some social scientists have regarded "cultural capital" as distinct from social capital. Generally, one may see culture as an asset in two ways. Some may see a cultural attitude, such as an emphasis on delayed gratification or a high esteem for education, as constructive and therefore useful. The late French sociologist

Pierre Bourdieu (1985) offered the second way of seeing culture as capital. Some cultural traits, according to Bourdieu, may be held in high regard in a society regardless of their practical value. Both senses of cultural capital can be relevant to migration issues. A home country tradition of literacy, for example, can promote upward mobility in the host country because people in the host country hold such a tradition in high esteem. Similarly, members of a host country may respond more positively to some cultural traits than others. Both of these senses of cultural capital, though, must face the problem of how groups maintain their cultures and adapt these to changing circumstances.

Robert S. Putnam (1993; 1995; 2000) used the term "social capital" to describe levels of social engagement, with an emphasis on organizational and institutional involvement. Although engagement in his sense could mean simply involvement in informal groups, he tended to concentrate on purposeful associations of people, whether those associations were bowling leagues, parent–teacher organizations, or political parties. The value of this engagement for individuals was implicit in Putnam's conceptualization, but he was chiefly concerned with engagement as an asset for groups or for societies. When people join bowling leagues, for example, this connects them to each other and promotes cooperation and collaboration that will be beneficial for their communities. When parents become involved in parent–teacher organizations, this benefits the school. By extension, the kind of engagement Putnam described also benefitted individuals who would enjoy the fruits of good communities and good schools.

Putnam did consider normative aspects of social engagement, especially the norm of trust. He argued that involvement in social groups, clubs, and organizations creates environments of trust and cooperation to promote collective action. In his controversial findings on community diversity, Putnam (2007) found lower levels of trust among people living in racially and ethnically diverse communities. Whether this is necessarily a result of diverse communities is open to question. Presumably, the reason heterogeneous populations have lower levels of trust is that they are less likely to engage with one another in the informal and formal groups that Putnam has seen as sources of social capital. There are arguably bases of cooperation and communication other than race or ethnicity. Moreover, Putnam's concentration on social capital as assets created by and for whole populations raises the distinct possibility that low levels of engagement and therefore trust in a heterogeneous town or city may be accompanied by high levels of engagement and trust within specific groups inside the town or city. This possibility calls attention to the relevance of the kinds of ties that may exist within and across group boundaries. Even in Putnam's version of social capital, then, with its emphasis on participation in formal and informal associations, social capital is implicitly embedded, to use a term from Portes (1998; also Portes and Sensenbrenner, 1993). Cultural expressions such as norms and values exist within the links created by social engagement. The associational involvements that Putnam emphasizes, then, should be considered as parts of broader social networks.

One of the clearest expressions of the network approach to social capital may be found in the work of James S. Coleman. In *Foundations of Social Theory* (1990) and other works, Coleman defines social capital in terms of network closure. Social capital exists, in Coleman's view, when there are close and closed networks among a set of individuals, promoting advantageous behavior. In Coleman's work, we can identify three primary parts to the generation of social capital. First, there are established patterns of interactions among persons. These are conceived in terms of network relations, which may occur within formal institutions such as the family or the school or in less formally structured settings such as the neighborhood. Second, there are normative orientations produced and maintained by patterns of interactions. Third, there are behavioral outcomes. Relationships among persons qualify as social capital when they produce and maintain normative orientations that lead to behavioral outcomes that enable individuals and groups to achieve desired goals. One of the virtues of the idea of social capital, then, is that it does link social structure, normative orientation, and action (Coleman 1990).

Along these lines, Grace Kao (2004) has described Coleman's

concept of social capital as consisting of three forms of resources that are aspects of the structure of relations among people. Kao applied to immigrants these three interrelated forms of resources: obligations and expectations, information channels, and social norms. Members of immigrant groups, according to Kao, tend to have relationships within their groups that involve more intense obligations and expectations because of relative isolation or alienation from the larger society. Because individuals communicate knowledge and understanding, the structure of relations among them can determine the kinds of information available to them. Members of immigrant groups have less access to the information available to natives, because of language and limited contact, and therefore rely heavily on flows of information along group lines. Relationships continually express and reinforce social norms, so that connections among immigrants can maintain a norm, such as trust, that applies specifically to group members. Thus, although social resources shape the experiences of all individuals, the resource of relationships within immigrant groups is especially important to immigrants. In contrast to the exclusively normative view of social capital as reducible to norms of trust, this relational approach emphasizes the advantageous arrangement of social networks.

Turning now to closer examination of how networks can provide assets, I look first at the psychological and cultural dimensions of networks by considering solidarity and norms as sources of assets provided by social relations. Then I consider the issues of how constraining or enabling relations may serve as assets, and I look at how network relationships may be informally and formally organized to serve individual and group goals.

How Do Social Resources Work?

In the social capital perspective, relationships among people are assets. For immigrants, this means that social connections can enable them to move from one place to another, to adapt to life in a new location, and to improve future prospects. Interpersonal ties can serve these ends by fostering solidarity: a strong sense of collective identity. Belonging to a group, such as an immigrant ethnic group, can give group members common interests and common identities, which encourage them to cooperate and assist each other (Portes, 1998). From a normative perspective, the cultural norms and values inherent in some relationships can result in cooperative, goal-oriented behavior.

Social Capital as Solidarity and as Norms

A solidarity view of social capital entails seeing identification with an immigrant or ethnic group as a potential asset for groups and group members. Language, memories of a shared ancestral homeland, and common experiences of migration may be sources of ethnic identification. Among refugee groups, political narratives of exile may be significant sources of shared experience. While isolation from the larger society may be a disadvantage in many ways, it can also contribute to an intense identification of group members with each other and promote mutual assistance.

As discussed earlier, some authors present social capital as essentially a matter of cultural norms, with emphasis on the norm of trust. Other cultural norms and values may also be regarded as leading to productive social behavior (see Zhou and Bankston, 1998; Hidalgo and Bankston, 2008). Where do cultural values come from and why would some groups manage to achieve relative academic or economic success on the basis of values? One answer might be that offered by Nathan Caplan and his co-authors in their work on Southeast Asian refugees (1989; 1991; 1992): immigrants bring cultural values with them from their ancestral country traditions and some of these values happen to be especially valuable in the context of adapting to life in the new country. One of the difficulties with this purely cultural version of social capital, though, is that it treats culture as floating in psychological space and simply imported around the world in the psyches of immigrants. However, norms and values are not just manifested in behavior; culture has to be grounded in patterns of social relations.

Cultures, moreover, do not travel unaltered from one location to another. In a metaphor that has achieved wide usage, Ann Swidler (1986) compared culture to a "toolkit," which contains many elements only some of which will be put to use, depending on the requirements of the environment. Further, people may put new "tools" in the kit. For example, extended families are often said to be one of the cultural norms of Vietnamese immigrants that have helped them adapt to life in the United States. However, Nazli Kibria (1993) convincingly argued that Vietnamese Americans have placed greater emphasis than people in Vietnam on extended families, due to the usefulness of family relations in adapting to life in a new land. Along these lines, Charles Tilly (1990) has pointed out that while social networks enable migration, migration also reshapes networks, and those reshaped networks produce new categorical identities and forms of cooperation.

Culture, like solidarity, has causes as well as consequences. In both cases, shared origin may be one of the causes, but not the only one. Common experiences of immigration and struggles to adjust to a new homeland can give rise to shared attitudes and perspectives, so that the culture of an immigrant group and its sense of identity derive from the process of migration, as well as from ancestral traditions, and the movement across boundaries can reshape those traditions. Further, solidarity and norms are interrelated. When members of a group identify intensely with it, they conform closely to the cultural orientations they see as characterizing the group. Solidarity and culture, though, exist within social structures. To begin to examine how social structures can guide thought and behavior, the next subsection considers how patterns of network connections can encourage or control individuals.

Enabling and Constraining Relations

Relations among immigrants, and others, may affect the pay-off of group membership in two ways. First, the relations may enable obtaining an end, such as when social ties result in information about employment, low-interest loans, or tutoring for young people. Second, the relations may constrain people (Zontini,

2010). The constraints may limit access to positions or benefits, a point to be discussed in greater depth in the subsection on problems with social capital. But constraining relations may also be assets, since they can enforce cooperation or discourage unproductive behavior.

Enabling and constraining relations can be considered as ways in which bonding and bridging network ties yield benefits and thereby become forms of capital. Bonding ties clearly constrain people. Being surrounded by those with whom one has close and frequent interactions and who have interactions with each other (high transitivity) limits an individual's freedom of action. Social relations are forms of social control and the tighter a set of social relations, the greater the social control. While social control may be negative, it can also have positive consequences. The solidarity, the sense of common identity, discussed in the previous section can be seen as a product and expression of control. Values such as trust, moreover, are rooted in control. A member of an immigrant group may, for example, be able to provide a loan to another member of the group on the basis of little or no collateral precisely because a tightly controlling set of relations guarantees repayment.

In addition, constraints have psychological value. Immigrants face special psychological challenges because they are by definition strangers in a strange land. The solidarity that provides common goals can also prevent group members from feeling lost and alone. The constraints of bonding ties also have behavioral consequences that may be positive. Control may be particularly important for young people because it can direct them toward productive and away from unproductive behavior.

The enabling relations of bonding ties are often the other side of the constraining relations. The control that guarantees repayment of a collateral-free loan can also make it easier for members of an immigrant group with a tight network to obtain those loans. The direction provided by an immigrant community to students may enable them to achieve as it channels them away from problematic forms of behavior. Bonding ties may also, though, enable individuals apart from the constraints. In Chapter 1, I pointed out that we may think of networks as lines of communication. Dense, intricately connected relations among people make possible the sharing of in-depth information, when that information is available to them.

While groups that are tightly bound with transitive, multiplex ties may share information in depth among group members, the very fact that they all have access to the same information means that it is difficult for them to obtain new information. An immigrant group may use close ties among members to achieve dominance in an industry, but it may be difficult for individuals in the group to move into new lines of work. Moreover, if group members have limited information or resources to share, constraining relations may provide individuals with privileged access to a very small body of opportunities.

Bonding ties, then, may enable to the extent that information or resources exist in an immigrant group's social network. Thus, Louise Ryan (2011) has argued that the dichotomy between bonding and bridging relations can be misleading and that in order to see social relations as forms of social capital one needs to consider what kinds of resources flow between social ties. Along similar lines, Michael Aguilera and Douglas Massey (2003) found that relationships with friends and relatives can improve the efficiency and effectiveness of job searches and lead to higher wages when those friends and relatives have previous experiences of immigration and of living in the United States.

The Aguilera and Massey findings suggest that if we look at networks as sets of potentially enabling relations, we may need to consider the ways in which bonding and bridging ties interact. Because intra-group bonding ties can involve the intense sharing of resources and information, they can be especially useful ways of enabling group members. The resources and information, though, must be accessible. If they come from the larger host society, they must be communicated through individuals with connections to that larger society. This brings up a critical point about bonding ties as ways of enabling immigrant group members. When resources are such that they can be created by those in a group, then a dense and tightly knit set of connections may be enabling. For example, if one thinks of family and community support for students as resources, one can see how an immigrant network can generate this through internal interactions. Immigrant groups cannot, however, initially generate their own knowledge about where to find opportunities in housing or employment. These sorts of resources come into the group through individuals who can act as bridges to the outside and make possible the enabling character of internal group relations. This is one of the reasons that "niches" come into existence. Individuals who have contacts with the surrounding society bring specific kinds of information and resources into an immigrant network, which may then share these among group members and make intensive use of limited access.

A wide but shallow social network is often considered primarily in terms of enabling relations. Indeed, this is the essence of Granovetter's "strength of weak ties" argument: the kinds of widespread links that people tend to have with relatively casual contacts can enable them to find the best possible opportunities. The "enabling" provided by contacts outside of a dense social network may offer a wide range, but it is also less intense than that provided within the network. Individuals who operate outside of an immigrant network are freer in the sense that they are less constrained by their obligations to other group members and by the solidarity of the group. By the same token, though, these individuals may be handicapped precisely by the limited support outside the group, since enabling and constraining are two sides of all social relations.

Ultimately, whether immigrant social relations can legitimately be taken as a form of social capital depends on what kinds of pay-offs are available. If an individual has access to the advantageous social structures of the host society, to socioeconomically privileged peer groups, to employment and finance, then an immigrant group may have little to offer that can enable that individual, and its constraints may limit life chances. If an individual does not have these kinds of access, then an immigrant network can offer valuable pay-offs through the sharing of resources and information about opportunities and constraints that encourage cooperation and discourage unproductive behavior.

Interpersonal Relations and Formal Organizations

Any set of social relations may consist of a set of people who have connections to each other, without any organizational base. As Scott Feld (1981) insightfully pointed out, though, not only do people tend to formalize their relations by creating organizations, but formal organizations provide focal points for social networks. An organization gives a social network a base of operations, defines people's links to each other, and helps provide groups with direction and goals. In addition, formal organizations can contribute to structuring relations along lines of authority (as in Figure 1.2), improving cooperation and efficiency in the flow of information.

Variations in the extent to which interpersonal relations are institutionally formalized can help us understand why interpersonal networks can work more effectively for some groups than for others. Because organizations have the potential to mobilize group members, to give network members clearly defined roles, and to direct networks toward goals, immigrants able to express social relations through organizations can promote individual and group interests more efficiently than those who lack explicit, formalized social structures.

What is Social Capital Invested In?

Capital is a resource for investment. Social capital consists of interconnections that can be invested in undertakings that pay off in some way. What are these undertakings? Some of the most important ones for immigrants include using social relations to raise financial capital, to create human capital, and to find opportunities and resources.

Social Capital in the Creation of Financial Capital

Limited accumulated wealth and lack of access to credit frequently handicap new immigrants in a market economy (Newberger et al.,

2004). Studies have consistently found that immigrants, especially low-income immigrants, are less likely to have bank accounts than natives are (Paulson et al., 2006; Rhine and Greene, 2006). Communities with large percentages of immigrants, moreover, show low rates of bank account ownership, even when socio-economic characteristics are held constant (Paulson et al., 2006). However, the access to formal sources of financial capital affects some immigrants more than others because some do have greater access and because different groups of immigrants have different financial capital needs.

Most contemporary immigrants fall into one of three occupational categories. First, there are low-skilled or semi-skilled labor migrants. This includes those engaged in agricultural work, construction work, and industries such as meat-packing and textiles. Second, there are skilled or highly educated migrants who arrive to take professional positions, such as physicians and nurses, engineers and technicians, and academics. Third, there are entrepreneurial immigrants, occupied in businesses such as small groceries, restaurants, and lodging establishments.

Access to financial capital poses the least problem for immigrants in the second category. While relatively recent arrival may often limit their credit, they enjoy the advantages of clearly defined places in the economy, comparatively good salaries, and often support from employers. Those in the first category, the low-skilled and semi-skilled laborers, need financial capital for expenses such as rent down-payments, travel expenses, and, if they seek to become homeowners, mortgages. Immigrants in the third category have the greatest need for capital in order to set themselves up in business.

Zhan et al. (2012) have found that many immigrants turn to informal financial sources because they do not have access to formal sources. Zhan and co-authors, for example, found that immigrants in the first occupational category must often turn to fee-charging check cashing services. Unable to build up credit, as well as paying exorbitantly for ordinary transactions, their capacity for investment in their own financial futures is severely limited.

In the absence of access to credit from banks and other host society institutions, social relations can frequently be sources of financial capital for setting up businesses. For the laboring immigrants and the entrepreneurial immigrants, trust and solidarity within social networks constitute credit. One of the differences between laboring immigrants and entrepreneurial immigrants, though, lies in the capacity of their respective social networks for raising funds and for making those funds available to group members.

The issue of how immigrant networks can develop pools of capital and act as financial sources for group members will be examined in more depth in Chapter 7. For now, it will suffice to give the brief example of Korean nail shop workers in the study of embeddedness and social support by Joong-Hwan Oh (2007). Although nail shop workers are not highly paid, those in this study received their pay and tips in cash. Each worker was expected by co-ethnics to put some of these earnings into rotating credit associations. Although the explicit purpose of these associations was primarily social, because these expressed and maintained group solidarity, they also had clear economic benefits as sources of financial capital and could enable workers to set up their own shops, which would in turn provide work in cooperative ethnic social settings.

Social Capital and Human Capital

James S. Coleman's 1988 article "Social Capital in the Creation of Human Capital" is one of the classic works in the social capital literature. In this article, Coleman discussed the concept of social capital and used it for an analysis of dropouts from high school. He argued that structural closure in a social network can establish obligations and expectations and maintain social norms. The structure of relations within families could direct children toward school completion and away from dropping out. Outside of the family, intergenerational closure (encompassing relationships among adults and children) had a further effect on educational attainment.

From the perspective of network structures, immigrants are often in complicated positions with regard to schools, the main institutions for acquiring human capital in contemporary society. As newcomers, immigrants may enjoy fewer links to schools than others do. Many immigrants have difficulty communicating with teachers and school officials due to the challenges of language. Immigrant parents may frequently feel intimidated by school bureaucracies. At the same time, though, the very fact that immigrant families are newcomers may intensify relationships among family members. Since intense parent–child relationships can encourage children to concentrate on school achievement, immigrant families may be unique sources for acquiring intergenerational human capital through social connections.

Beyond families, though, immigrant groups often have wider ethnically based social networks, which surround and support the families. Often organized around the formal organizations discussed in detail in Chapter 6, these wider immigrant networks can reinforce the direction and control of families, creating intergenerational closure not simply between parents and children, but among children and communities of adults.

In some respects, one might regard immigrant social capital as an alternative asset for accumulating human capital, as it is an alternative asset for accumulating financial capital. Min Zhou and I (1998) looked at a major substitutive aspect of immigrant social capital in the creation of human capital by considering social capital in the context of the segmented assimilation theory developed chiefly by Alejandro Portes. From the perspective of segmented assimilation theory, many contemporary immigrants settle in severely disadvantaged low-income areas, in which residents have little expectation of upward mobility, resulting in discouragement and alienation among young people, attitudes that students communicate to each other in and out of schools. In this setting, supportive relationships among immigrant families and within immigrant communities may mobilize adults and young people to promote educational achievement and attainment and thereby substitute for social assets not otherwise available.

The substitutes for social assets may not, in fact, be limited to immigrants in economically disadvantaged locations and situations. Although middle-class young people do not face the challenges of the poor, the former may also experience age segregation and youth cultures that are suspicious of those who study hard and apply themselves in schools. Even in relatively advantaged socioeconomic settings, then, intergenerational closure between immigrant parents and children and among immigrant children who share the mobility orientations of their elders may promote the accumulation of human capital.

Social Relations and Opportunities

Although Coleman's 1988 article concentrated on expectations and obligations and social norms as ways that social capital can create human capital, he also identified information channels as ways in which networks can produce assets. I have discussed the idea of networks as lines of communication in Chapter 1. Primarily through lines of communication, social relations can be investments in finding and obtaining opportunities. This differs from the network as a means of mobilization to generate financial capital. Accessing and mobilizing social capital may, however, be connected. For example, the movement of Asian Indian immigrants into the motel industry in the United States involved employing networks to find opportunities, in locating where available motels may be located, and in raising financial capital to invest in those motels (see Dhingra, 2010; 2012).

Networks lie at the core of access to many opportunities in any society. One of the reasons that occupational niches come to be dominated by kin groups or ethnic groups is that people tend to give preferential treatment to their relatives and co-ethnics. This type of preferential treatment can be both a disadvantage and an advantage for immigrants, depending on what opportunities are sought and what opportunities exist within network lines of communication and distribution. Networks, then, deny access just as they permit access, one of the problems with social capital views of networks.

Problems with Immigrant Networks as Sources of Social Capital

As described in Chapter 2, social capital consists of patterns of relationships among people that can serve as assets for investment, on the analogy of financial capital. This analogy is theoretically problematic. Financial capital consists of specific quantities for investment. If I have $500 to invest, I may invest wisely or foolishly or my investment may pay off or not depending on changes in the market. But my capital is clearly identifiable and neither its nature nor its amount depends on the outcome of the investment. Whether relationships are seen as constituting "capital," though, often depends precisely on what the relationships produce (although the question of "negative social capital" even makes this observation problematic).

The idea of social capital may be criticized as a tautology precisely because a social network is an asset when it produces desirable results. This is only part of a deeper theoretical difficulty with the idea, though. We know where we can find financial capital: it is the amount that is invested. We also know where to find human capital: it is a definable skill or credential. Social capital, though, is emergent in nature. It is not any specific quantity held by individuals or by groups, but is produced through the interactions among individuals in their interactions. Moreover, the consequences of group interactions are contextual. Interactions within patterns of relationships that are advantageous in some settings may not be advantageous in others (Bankston and Zhou, 2002).

Adaptation or Upward Mobility?

The question of whether social relationships defined by race or ethnicity promote adaptation or upward mobility has a long heritage. In their classic work *The City* (1925), Robert E. Park and his co-authors described newly arrived immigrants as characterized primarily by their disadvantages. The immigrants' unfamiliarity with their host society and their familiarity with their own language and customs led them to establish their homes in dense ethnic concentrations. These ethnic concentrations provided them with psychological and emotional supports, but not opportunities for upward mobility.

A substantial literature, as well as common sense, supports the idea that bonding ties within ethnic networks are investments in the psychological security of group members. Among older immigrants, in particular, being part of an ethnic community can be an effort to reproduce the ancestral country heritage in the host country (Park et al., 2012; Yoo and Zipay, 2012). The emotional benefits of networks can also flow to younger immigrants, though. Gellis (2003) found that Vietnamese immigrants with ethnic networks extending beyond kin showed reduced depression scores over time.

This view of immigrant networks as providing support and security is connected to the idea that ethnic networks can provide means of "getting by" rather than "getting ahead," of adapting rather than thriving. Here, the social capital argument draws on one of the longstanding debates about the benefits of immigrant communities and networks: by supporting immigrants and providing supports and security, do these isolate them from potential opportunities in the larger society? On this issue, Bram Lancee (2012) found, using longitudinal data, that bridging ties of immigrants with German natives were related to advantageous employment, while bonding ties among immigrants had no effect. Lancee concluded that his findings supported "isolation" arguments about ethnic ties rather than "closure" arguments.

One answer to the question of whether immigrant networks can supply both adaptation and upward mobility may lie in the structure of those networks. Specifically, an economically differentiated structure may make a network a source of economic opportunity, as well as cultural comfort. Along these lines, Portes and Manning (1986) and Portes and Jensen (1987) have emphasized the importance of economic differentiation in creating a viable ethnic community. They have maintained that ethnic communities can promote successful adaptation for their members by placing the members in interconnected social roles as employers, employees, and consumers. Similarly, Zhou (1992) has argued that New York's Chinatown has been a successful ethnic enclave because of its varied, interdependent institutions. However, this leaves open the question of why some immigrant groups are sufficiently internally differentiated to create ethnically based economies that will lead to mobility, while others are not. Moreover, the very fact that different kinds of social networks may produce different kinds of benefits points out the ambiguity in the pay-off provided by social capital.

The Problem of "Negative Social Capital"

The possibility that immigrant networks may contribute to isolation instead of productive closure raises the problem of "negative social capital." Financial capital is a resource regardless of whether it is well invested or pays off as expected. Social capital, though, is often defined as ties among people that yield benefits. In describing structures of immigrant social ties as "capital," are we engaging in tautology or can we accept the seemingly contradictory notion of "negative social capital"? Regardless of the concerns we might have about it, this is a term with a fairly extensive history in recent decades, used by prominent researchers such as Patricia Fernández Kelly (1995) to refer to network ties that have results that are disadvantageous from some perspective. These results can be of various types, though. One type is the "capital" that can be invested in adaptation to an environment, rather than in mobility. When the environment itself is seen as disadvantageous, such as a low-income neighborhood, then the investment yields results that might ultimately be seen as undesirable: it promotes "getting by" in an underprivileged setting, rather than "getting ahead."

Another sense in which social capital might be understood as "negative" is if the very benefits a cooperative social network yields are seen as undesirable. For example, in studying Latino and Asian gang members, Pih et al. (2008) found that these gangs have become economic entities and provide valuable networks for financial opportunities. Indeed, effective criminal activities in general may depend on tight, cooperative bonds among those involved in them. Is this "negative" or "positive" social capital?

Weil et al. (2012) offer an interesting variant on ways in which the kinds of ties associated with social capital may be both positive and negative. In looking at people who experienced Hurricane Katrina, these authors find that those who were more involved in social networks initially experienced negative consequences because they had greater obligations than social isolates toward others. However, the more involved also recovered from their stressful experiences more readily than those who were relatively isolated. Extending the insights of Weil et al. to immigrants, we can see how the idea that social capital can be negative as well as positive can give us a greater understanding of the complicated effects of social networks. Immigrants who have dense, highly supportive networks not only receive advantages from those networks, but also have the disadvantages of obligations. Along these lines, Min Zhou and I (Zhou and Bankston, 2001) found that young Vietnamese women in the United States often perceived their own ties to family and community as burdensome and demanding because of the obligations entailed by the gender roles imposed by network ties. However, the same obligations that burdened the young women also often encouraged school achievement.

The insider–outsider distinctions created by social networks also mean that these networks may make some of those in immigrant ethnic groups into relative outsiders precisely because of the strong and closed connections. In our work on how Vietnamese American community networks have promoted school achievement, Min Zhou and I noted not only that closely knit networks demand conformity and place heavy obligations on their members, but also that those in immigrant groups who do not conform and are not tightly integrated into family and community relations face rejection. We attributed the tendency of immigrant young people to bifurcate into underachievers and overachievers to the support and direction given to those who fit into the networks of the ethnic community and the rejection experienced by those who did not (Bankston and Zhou, 1997).

The definition of social capital as network ties that produce positive outcomes is problematic, then, because the positive nature is itself contingent and relative. We may see supports that help people to survive in a disadvantaged socioeconomic setting as positive precisely because these supports enable them to survive or negative because the supports maintain them in that setting. We may see the pay-off of networks as undesirable for others or for the society as a whole or even as ultimately self-destructive, as in the case of networks of individuals involved in criminal activities. Finally, the positive and negative consequences of cooperative social action may be inextricably entangled or different sides of the same arrangement.

Capital, Competition, and Conflict

Social Resources and Group Competition

Like financial capital and human capital, social capital is an asset for investment in the competition for advantages. Like other forms of capital, also, social capital is inherently ambiguous from the perspective of moral or ethical values. Even when networks function to provide benefits for individuals or groups, they do not provide benefits for everyone and they may often be understood as providing benefits for some at the expense of others. Looking at voluntary associations, often considered a key element and indicator of social capital along the lines described by Robert Putnam, Hajdeja Iglic (2010) has found that the particularized trust built up within associations tends to diminish the tolerance of members for outsiders. A network in which all members are tightly bound to each other is one in which in-group relations are much stronger than relations with others. A social capital model of providing resources and seeking opportunities, then, replaces the idea of a society and economy composed of competing individuals with one composed of competing groups.

Following Charles Tilly (1998; 2005), Douglas S. Massey (2007) identifies opportunity hoarding as one of the main mechanisms for perpetuating inequality among categories and groups of people. "*Opportunity hoarding* occurs," Massey writes, "when one social group restricts access to a scarce resource, whether through outright denial or by exercising monopoly control that requires out-group members to pay rent in return for access. Either way, opportunity hoarding is enabled through a *socially defined process of exclusion*" (p. 6; italics in the original). Whether this exclusion is desirable or undesirable depends on whether one takes the perspective of those hoarding the opportunities or that of those being excluded from them.

We can take self-employment within immigrant groups as an example of one way in which social capital may enable the hoarding of resources. There is a finite demand for small stores. If immigrants work together with their co-ethnics to make funds for opening small stores available to insiders, they are creating an advantage over outsiders, especially native-born minority outsiders who may have as little access to formal institutions of credit as the immigrants, who achieve a competitive advantage in entrepreneurship. The same logic also follows for access to jobs or other resources: preferentially hiring or giving information to insiders by definition gives advantages over outsiders.

Even when opportunity hoarding is not a conscious process, the flow of information along network lines (see Figure 1.3) means that networks implicitly hoard information about opportunities. Thus, social capital flows along lines of advantage and reinforces advantages. Although we typically think of network advantages in terms of "old boy networks," these advantages accrue to any group that shares privileged information based on the similarities of group members (McDonald, 2011).

Group competition, with some groups hoarding opportunities, extends to the accumulation of human capital through social capital. In looking at how ethnic social networks can promote the academic achievement of young people in immigrant groups, for example, researchers essentially examine how immigrant group networks can concentrate social assets on young people in their own groups and propel these young people ahead of others in an educational system based on competition (see Zhou and Bankston, 1998).

In addition to giving network members advantages over outsiders, network connections may, in some cases, enable some immigrants to exploit fellow group members. In the previous section, I pointed out that the networks that provide benefits to group members also impose burdens and obligations on them. In many situations both the benefits and the burdens are reciprocal and equally shared. In others, though, even within the networks the burdens may fall more heavily on some and the benefits may accrue more to others. Low-cost or free labor provided by co-ethnics and family members can help immigrant businesses succeed, but this can often require sacrifices from the workers.

I have pointed out that the literature suggests that immigrant networks may be most effective at enabling group members to move up rather than get by when the networks are internally differentiated and involve individuals in different and often unequal positions. The issue of immigrant networks providing upward mobility, then, raises the question of whether they provide mobility for all, or simply for the employers who hold the greatest portfolios of social capital, in the form of access to cheap labor and guaranteed markets, through privileged positions in the system of ethnic social connections.

The "Balkanization" Problem

Since social capital substitutes competition among groups for competition among individuals, it raises the possibility of a society divided among groups with high internal solidarity. Putnam (2007) found some evidence that ethnically diverse communities can show lower levels of overall trust and cohesion than homogeneous communities. This may be the consequence of the breakdown of ethnically based solidarity, so that individuals live in relative isolation among others with whom they have little in common. However, a low overall level of trust and cohesion across groups may also be the consequence of high trust and cohesion within groups, so that interaction among networks competing to accumulate and hoard resources is limited and uneasy.

Competition for resources and the categorization of people into in-groups and out-groups are common explanations for interethnic social distance and conflict (see, for example, the discussion in Esses et al., 2001). Social capital ideas imply that the ability of groups to compete for scarce resources depends on strong connections and strong identifications within groups, as well as sharp lines of distinction among groups. Thus, the use of social relations as assets can divide a society into multiple, competing sets of people. This does not necessarily produce conflict. Ethnic specialization, for example, may mean that members of an immigrant group use their social relations to thrive in a particular niche that is not sought by members of other groups. Even this can mean that interaction with outsiders is limited to customer–patron relationships, though, and all more intense interactions are limited to insiders. In other circumstances, the insider–outsider distinction associated with tightly knit immigrant networks may actually be associated with intergroup conflict. Jennifer Lee (1999), for example, has discussed how differing ethnic advantages among Jewish, Korean, and African American entrepreneurs produce both exclusion from economic niches and social distance across groups. Thus, intergroup mistrust and social distance can accompany the in-group cooperation and solidarity that produce social capital.

These instances of the often ambiguous nature of social capital do not mean that one should reject the view that patterns of connections among people may provide important assets for both groups and individuals. The instances should, however, caution us against taking social capital as a panacea, and against interpreting differences in economic and educational outcomes across immigrant groups and between immigrants and native-born minority members as simply consequences of relatively effective or ineffective network characteristics.

3

Networks Within and Across Nations

Researchers in immigration have long recognized that migration takes place through networks. A small number of pioneers may move alone to locations previously unknown to them, where they make their way as complete strangers. Most potential immigrants, though, hear about opportunities in other locations from neighbors, friends, and family members. In migrating, they tend to move along the lines established by earlier immigrants with whom they have some social connection. Immigrants who settle in a location or who move among locations for purposes of work draw other immigrants after them. Immigration, then, begins with social networks within countries of origin, follows network lines across boundaries, and results in immigrant networks within countries of destination.

The social patterns underlying immigration vary among migrant groups, and they vary because the networks within nations and across nations are shaped by wider social, economic, and political contexts and conditions in countries and between countries. In this chapter, I look at those wider contexts and conditions. In order to make this examination as concrete as possible, I will concentrate on the examples of four major immigrant groups: Mexicans, Koreans, Vietnamese, and Filipinos. Comparing the influences on the network forms of these cases can clarify why different immigrant networks take differing forms, offering varied assets to group members, and it will make it possible to generalize beyond these selected examples by using them as points of reference.

Contexts of Exit and Reception

If social networks shape migration and the lives of immigrants, what shapes social networks? What influences how those networks function? These are questions of context and concern the determinants of social action in the country of origin and the nature of the connections between the country of origin and the country of destination. Specifically, they concern historical events and consequent social structures in the home country; historical connections between the home country and the destination, including the role of race and ethnicity as contexts affecting the acceptance of immigrants, and policy issues such as the legal status of immigrants; and country of origin social structures, such as educational background of immigrants and urban or rural origin of immigrants. Figure 3.1 gives an approximation of these contextual influences at the left of the figure and then plots out how these affect immigrant settlement and networks. This figure shows the major background features of geographic proximity between sending and receiving countries; historic relations between the countries, and country of origin social structures, as direct influences on interpersonal ties across borders; geographic mobility of immigrants; and migration and settlement patterns. Where and how people settle are also shaped by mobility and by cross-border links. In turn cross-national ties, mobility, and settlement affect the network forms of families, broader communities, and organizations. The interconnected network forms, in their turn, result in varied types and levels of control and cooperation among network members and in variations in the flow of information. In order to examine clearly how these interrelated phenomena serve as sources of networks as social resources, the following sections will look at how they have worked among several major immigrant groups.

Immigrants from Mexico

For immigrants from Mexico, the central fact about contexts of exit and reception is a geographic proximity that makes potential

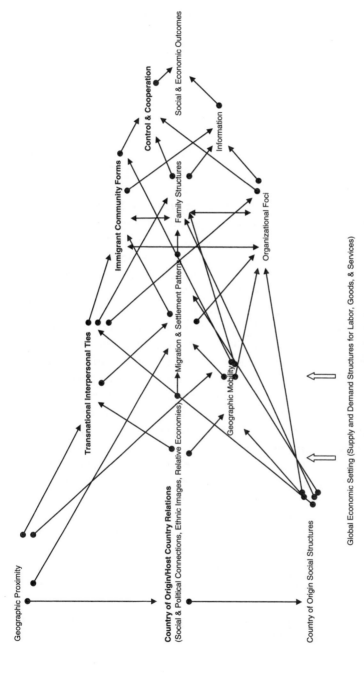

Figure 3.1 Influences on Immigrant Network Structures and Social Outcomes

migrants especially responsive to Latin American push factors and to the pull of economic demand in the United States, and creates continuous cross-border networks. The second major contextual characteristic is that the Latin American countries that are physically part of the same land mass as the United States are much poorer than the northern neighbor. This makes the former a ready source of an inexpensive and highly flexible labor force for the latter.

The poverty of Latin America relative to North America has been fairly constant, but the seriousness of this poverty has changed over time. In Mexico, the country that sends the largest number of immigrants to the U.S. of any country and the source of the overwhelming majority of Latin American immigrants, a decline in the price of oil produced a debt crisis beginning about 1982. As a consequence, legal Mexican immigration northward increased rapidly, from a little over 621,000 in the decade 1970–9 to over 1 million in the 1980s. In 1994, a second economic shock, the devaluation of the peso, caused dramatic inflation and a decline in Mexican living standards. In response to the economic problems, over 2.75 million Mexicans immigrated legally to the United States in the 1990s, and from 2000 to 2005 the United States received an average of 200,000 legal permanent residents from Mexico every year (United States Department of Homeland Security, 2006).

As the numbers grew, so did the dispersion. Immigrants from Latin America, and especially from Mexico, spread to new destinations, places that until the end of the twentieth century had been destinations for few immigrants. In Figure 3.1, this is represented as high geographic mobility leading to dispersed settlement. The pull part of this new destination phenomenon was the rise of industries requiring relatively low-cost labor with enough geographic mobility to respond to demand in widely spread locations. Some researchers have argued too that the movement to new locations was also pushed by policy and labor market changes in the United States, such as saturation of older immigrant labor markets, official hostility to immigration in older receiving areas, and a hardening of border controls by U.S. Immigration that deflected immigration from the Southwest (Massey and Capoferro, 2008; Light, 2006).

Proximity and inequality translate readily into geographic mobility. While places of origin within Mexico and its southern neighbors are fairly stable geographically, since migrants are moving out of existing communities, the migrants are frequently continually moving to new places within the United States, and these facts affect the nature and use of network connections, or, in the terms of Figure 3.1, transnational interpersonal ties. As discussed in Chapter 4, Flores-Yeffal and Aysa-Lastra (2011) found that people from the same place of origin in Mexico (or *paisanos)* were especially important at the beginning of a migratory flow from a location, and that immigrants often relied more on strong ties with family and friends as more migrants from the same place arrived.

In this case, and in the cases of the groups that follow, we can see concrete examples of what Doreian and Conti (2012) identify as the shaping of network structure by social context and spatial structure. The high degree of mobility means that Latin American migrant flows to new destinations frequently intensify the importance of networks characterized by weak ties, rather than the strong bounded ties that James Coleman and others have generally associated with social capital. Moreover, while *paisanos* may be important for the initial cross-border movement, secondary migration, which may weaken links among *paisanos*, tends to make Latin American immigrant networks channels for limited, if frequently useful, information and limits the control and support implicit in these networks. Accordingly, Chávez et al. (2006) found that Mexican migrant seasonal farm workers often show low levels of trust toward both other Hispanics and non-Hispanics.

The ready mobility tends to maintain loose, relatively weak networks among Latin American immigrants so that they can get information about where resources such as jobs and housing may be found, but these network forms function less well for mobilizing to generate entrepreneurial resources or to provide tight controls and supports to promote upward mobility on the part of younger people. The mobility and proximity also contribute to another major influence on Latin American network structure: the vast numbers of undocumented immigrants. While the undocumented rely on co-ethnics to find jobs and places of settlement, the fact that so many lack legal status further contributes to the instability of networks.

In terms of Figure 3.1, transnational ties, geographic mobility, and settlement patterns affect network patterns (in communities, families, and organizations), with consequences for control and cooperation and information flows. Contributing to the fluidity of Mexican migration, much of it is seasonal in character, and (U.S. border controls permitting) involves people who move back and forth as they search for work in the North and return to communities in Mexico. The vast body of research generated by the Mexican Migration Project (http://mmp.opr.princeton.edu/home-en.aspx) headed by Douglas S. Massey and Jorge Durand Arp-Nisen, gathered through interviews and surveys among Mexican immigrants in the United States and in sending communities in Mexico, has documented the extensive transnational ties between the U.S. and Mexico and the enormous impact of continuing migration on the social structures of Mexico, as well as on Mexican immigrants in the North. While these ties are important for back-and-forth movement, limited economic opportunities in the North, difficulties of transnational movements created by U.S. immigration policy, and resource-poor communities on both sides of the border tend to make transnational ties tenuous and limit their value as resources. Along similar lines, Menjívar (2000) has documented the even more tenuous nature of transnational ties among Salvadoran immigrants across the whole of Mexico, as well as across the U.S.–Mexican border.

Finally, ethnicity has played a role in maintaining a context of reception (country of origin/host country relations) for people from Mexico and Central America. Ethnic stereotypes of Mexicans and Central Americans have long been a part of North American popular preconceptions. Since mainland Latin Americans have been historically heavily occupied in manual labor, such as agricultural work, this has influenced conscious and unconscious opinions about what kind of work is "Mexican work." Even in recent times, as the widespread use of laborers from the South has led many North Americans of other ethnicities to develop positive images of Latin American workers, those images still tend to be associated with manual labor (Wortham et al., 2009). It is difficult to quantify the extent to which ethnic stereotyping constrains economic opportunities for Mexicans and Central Americans, but it clearly tends to channel unskilled and semi-skilled occupations into the flow of resources moving along their lines of social connections.

Korean Immigrants

Although immigrants began to arrive from Korea in the 1950s, large-scale Korean migration began only following the change of U.S. immigration laws in 1965, which altered relations between the United States and many Asian nations. Numbers of Korean immigrants more than doubled in the late 1960s, rising from 10,179 individuals between 1960 and 1965 to 25,618 between 1966 and 1970. Although many of the earliest post-1965 immigrants came on occupational visas, after 1976 family reunification, the most common basis for being legally admitted to the United States in general, became the main way in which Koreans were admitted. This gave official reinforcement through transnational family ties. As a result, Korean migration increased sharply during the 1980s, with 172,851 Koreans entering legally between 1986 and 1990. Although Korean immigration dropped following the 1988 Seoul Olympic Games and the rise of the Korean economy, numbers of immigrants began to rise again following an economic crisis in 1997 (Yoon, 2012).

In 1962, the Korean government adopted policies to encourage emigration in order to lessen population pressure and to seek remittances from abroad. The Korean immigrants who took advantage of the Korean and U.S. policies favoring migration initially tended to be well-educated, white-collar, middle-class professionals. During the peak years of the 1980s, though, Korean immigrants from a wider range of socioeconomic backgrounds began to arrive in the United States (Yoon, 2012). Nevertheless, human capital remained comparatively high, so that clerical and managerial abilities were fairly widespread. Because English is not widely spoken in Korea, though, those leaving Korea generally had little English even when they held many other forms of human capital.

One of the country of origin social structures that is of particular importance for understanding Korean immigrant networks, especially from the perspective of networks as means of generating assets, concerns religion. Although the historic religious traditions of Korea are Buddhist, Korean Christianity has grown rapidly in South Korea since the end of the Korean War. By 2005, about 30 percent of Koreans were self-declared Protestants or Roman Catholics, with a heavy majority of Protestants, and Protestant forms of congregationalism and evangelization have also influenced Buddhists (Grayson, 2009). Korean international immigrants, then, come to their country of destination with an experience of religious organizations as key social institutions and with an established pattern of these organizations receiving newcomers and making converts.

Societal prejudice and discrimination, as well as language barriers and the difficulty of transferring Korean educational credentials to the United States, have imposed serious disadvantages on Koreans in the labor market (Min, 1996), but disadvantages that differ from those of Latin American immigrants. Mexicans have been channeled into the bottom of this labor market, while Koreans have found themselves at its outer margins. The large influx of immigrants from Korea in recent years means that there are many who are still relative outsiders to the American society and economy but insiders to their own co-ethnic groups. The outsider status of Koreans has encouraged those in these groups to maintain close, dense, cooperative, and constraining ties.

Without access to many positions in the larger economy but with close links to other ethnic group members, Korean immigrants have been uniquely situated to move into marginal positions of small-scale self-employment. Over the past few decades, Koreans have had one of the highest rates of self-employment among immigrant groups, largely in small businesses serving minority neighborhoods in the United States. Their ethnic networks provided the means for these relative outsiders to take these marginal positions, while developments in the country of destination opened up places for them.

Vietnamese and Other Southeast Asians

People in North America of mainland Southeast Asian origin, most of whom are Vietnamese, arrived as part of a refugee wave. From 1975 through 2009, a total of 1,773,733 people from Southeast Asian arrived in the United States as refugees, 770,961 of them from Vietnam. During this time, approximately 887,000 people entered from Vietnam alone officially classified as immigrants or legal permanent residents. For all practical purposes, those designated as immigrants were part of the same refugee movement.

The Southeast Asians were breaking with their homelands to a greater extent than most other immigrants. Although mail did move back and forth and remittances from abroad became a major part of the Vietnamese economy, for most of the period from 1975 through the 1990s, Southeast Asian immigrants were essentially cut off from their former homelands. As refugees or as immigrants arriving under special government programs, their resettlement initially received substantial bureaucratic direction. At first, the U.S. government followed a policy of attempting to scatter Southeast Asian refugees around the country, in order to promote assimilation. However, ethnic concentrations soon emerged. This was to some extent due to the fact that it was easier to relocate refugees together where housing was available and easier to provide services to people in identifiable locations. It was also due, though, to secondary migration by new arrivals seeking the company and support of co-ethnics. This "scattering and reconcentration" pattern of geographic settlement had implications for immigrant network structures. While some nationally recognized ethnic communities did arise, for the most part Southeast Asians formed small ethnic residential centers all around the country, each of which had family and friendship ties to centers in other locations. Essentially, for Southeast Asians the United States became a nationwide network of Southeast Asian communities, each of which had its own internal network relations.

The Vietnamese, who constituted the majority of the Southeast Asian refugee groups, were able to construct the most coherently interdependent communities. As Min Zhou and I (1998) described these, each community became a center of closely knit ethnic ties. This does not mean that these communities were without conflict. As almost anyone with a family can testify, close ties are often the most fraught with tensions and conflicts. But it does mean that relatively high degrees of support and control characterized most Vietnamese communities in the United States.

The smaller Southeast Asian refugee groups, including Lao, Hmong, and Cambodians (Khmer), have shown patterns of interconnected communities around the United States similar to those of the Vietnamese. However, these smaller groups have generally been somewhat less organized than the Vietnamese and have had somewhat more difficulty in establishing bridging ties to the surrounding society. These differences can be attributed to variations in contexts of exit among the refugee groups. The first wave of Vietnamese refugees to arrive in the late 1970s often came from relatively privileged segments of their society. Among them were generals, police officers, military officers, employees of American agencies and corporations, and members of the elite classes. These first arrivals could establish the groundwork for creating ethnic networks among later arrivals (Zhou et al., 2001).

Later arrivals, especially from Laos and Cambodia, were less likely than the first wave to come from urban backgrounds. Over one-third of the Lao, half of the Hmong, and 40 percent of Cambodians who arrived in the 1980s barely had an elementary education (Zhou et al., 2001). Contextual characteristics, then, limited the ability of the smaller Southeast Asian groups to translate network connections into assets. These characteristics included fewer elite pioneers and less human capital for use by group members. The forms of the networks they established in the new country were similar to those of the Vietnamese, but the content of these networks was less advantageous.

Religious institutions brought from the country of origin and adapted to the country of destination have been important centers of social organization. Catholic churches, especially among the Vietnamese, and Buddhist temples have become focal points for organizing social networks and maintaining ethnic identities. The reconstituting of Southeast Asian communities in small clusters around the United States has made possible the establishment of these home country religious organizations and, in turn, the organizations have given institutional form to Southeast Asian social networks.

Filipinos

Perhaps the most distinctive aspect of the contexts of exit and reception for Filipino immigrants concerns their extensive and intensive historic association with the United States, and the effect of this association on social structures in the Philippines (see Figure 3.1). The United States established its domination over the Philippines in the late nineteenth century. American business interests dominated the economy of the Philippines. American administrators, often motivated by genuine if frequently con-descending idealism, created an extensive public school system, founded the University of the Philippines on the American higher education model, and constructed roads and public buildings. Even after Philippine independence, following World War II, political, economic, and cultural links between the two countries remained strong (Bankston, 2006). This close connection between the two countries has been an intimate part of the context of exit as an influence on the networks of Filipino migrants.

The public education system dating from the American colonial period endowed many Filipinos with high levels of human capital that were immediately transferable to the American context. Instruction above the sixth grade is generally in English in the Philippines and credentials are comparable to those of American institutions. While Mexicans migrated to fill demand for workers at the bottom of the socioeconomic scale and Koreans had to create their own opportunities at the margins of the labor market, a substantial segment of historically recent Filipino immigrants migrated to fill demand for highly skilled professions. Nurses were a particularly notable part of this segment, encouraged by U.S. legislation that gave special opportunities to those who could help meet the nursing shortage. Nursing became a stereotypical occupation for Filipino American women, but during the 1990s and 2000s, American recruiters were seeking other professionals, such as teachers, from the Philippines to meet labor market demands (Bankston, 2006).

An even larger segment of Filipino immigrants came from marriage. Spouses of military personnel made up about half of the immigrants from the Philippines to the United States between 1946 and 1965 (Reimers, 1985). As other migrants increased in numbers, spouses continued to flow from the Philippines. Even the 1991 closing of U.S. bases did not end the established pattern of spousal migration. In 1998, for example, 7,697 individuals born in the Philippines were admitted to the United States as spouses of U.S. citizens, the single largest category of all Filipino legal migrants (United States Department of Justice, Immigration and Naturalization Service, 2000: table 8). Accordingly, marriage outside the group was extremely common for Filipino immigrants, a characteristic with important implications for the workings of transnational ties. The fact that Filipino spousal immigrants were mainly women indicates that relations between countries include gender relations between representatives of those countries and the fact that gender relations play an essential part in transnational connections.

Even though the Philippines has such long and close historical links with the United States, immigration from the Philippines, like immigration from other countries, increased sharply after the 1965 immigration law changes, so that Filipino Americans are also largely a post-1965 group. However, immigration before 1965 established some channels for the more recent influx. Marriage migrants and professional migrants together became the bases for international family networks that brought in still more migrants. In fiscal year 2011, 36 percent of legal permanent residents admitted to the United States from the Philippines came in under family-sponsored preferences and 51 percent came in as immediate relatives of U.S. citizens. By comparison, 22 percent of worldwide legal permanent residents were admitted under the family-sponsored preferences and 43 percent were admitted as immediate relatives of U.S. citizens (United States Department of Homeland Security, 2012: table 11). Post-1965 American immigration policy favored migrants with U.S. family members under the family reunification preference, but Filipinos, with cross-national family networks created by the particular type of historic closeness between the two countries, made especially heavy use of migration along lines of family connections.

Undocumented immigration also followed from transnational family-based ties. Given their English-language abilities, their general familiarity with American culture, and their family members in North America, Filipinos who wish to migrate but are not admitted are well placed to overstay visas, if they can get these for purposes of visiting relatives or general tourism. Consistently, throughout the 2000s, only Mexico and the Central American nations, with their physical proximity to the U.S., exceeded the Philippines, with its social proximity, in numbers of unauthorized immigrants. In 2010, an estimated 280,000 unauthorized Filipino immigrants resided in the United States (Hoefer et al., 2011).

The transnational, usually family-based networks that bring Filipinos to the United States have their opposite side in the phenomenon of the *balikbayan* (roughly, "national returnees" in Tagalog). U.S. legal residents and citizens regularly return to visit their relatives in the island nation. Their remittances form a major part of the Philippine economy. The transnational networks of Filipinos may be as extensive as those of Mexican immigrants, even though the geographical distance is much greater. Transnational networks, for all groups, enable the back-and-forth movement of goods and people, as well as initial migration and settlement. Their differences concern contextual influences, especially legality and other matters of migration status. The more a group is composed of legal migrants, the easier the cross-border transfers.

Although there are some Filipino American residential concentrations, notably in the Los Angeles area, the professional occupations of many Filipino immigrants, the high level of inter-marriage, and the abilities of Filipino Americans to negotiate North American culture and institutions tend to make settlement patterns widely dispersed and often less immediately visible than those of many other groups with recent immigrant origins. It might seem that the contextual factors make Filipino networks useful for movement across national boundaries, but have little value as assets within the United States. The institutional cores of many immigrant groups are less obvious in the case of Filipinos. In particular, the religious organizations that are important to Koreans and Vietnamese play a much smaller part among the mainly mainstream Catholic Filipinos. However, as I'll discuss in Chapter 6, Filipino networks often do have institutional founda-tions, such as "Fil-Am" organizations. Moreover, these networks often provide support groups that are important even to such externally assimilated Philippine immigrants as professionals and out-married Filipinos.

In general, the network patterns resulting from the contextual influences on Filipinos tend to include strong but often geographi-cally widespread family ties at the center. These are widespread not only because they derive from transnational links but also because within the United States Filipinos are generally dispersed. Non-family networks are often localized, based on informal friendship circles and on clubs. These non-family networks tend to be weaker than those of more residentially concentrated immi-grant origin groups. While they provide emotional support and symbolic identity, they offer less control and direction than, say, the Vietnamese communities I have described. Both the friendship circles and the stronger family networks can provide information, such as financial advice and where to find jobs. This kind of infor-mation can be especially useful for the undocumented. Moreover, Filipinos have exceptionally strong and numerous bridging ties to connect group members with the larger society through marriage and professional connections. Although Filipino immigrants do have identifiable ethnic networks, these networks are less inten-sive than those of many other immigrant groups, since Filipino ties exist among people who know each other chiefly through relationships at single family, friendship, or organizational levels, and Filipinos often have broader links to people outside of their ethnically based "catnets."

Networks in the Global Economy

The global economic setting conditions how contexts of exit and reception shape the ways immigrants move across borders, settle, and form social networks. Understanding how proximity, historic links between countries, and country of origin social structures result in particular types of immigration and immigrant communities requires thinking about markets for labor, goods, and services.

Immigration has always been part of the global economy, and immigrant social structures have always operated under the influence of global economic forces, as represented at the bottom of Figure 3.1. At the time of the great wave of American immigration at the end of the nineteenth and the beginning of the twentieth century, the northern European nations had reached full maturity as industrial powers and become centers of capital and investment. North America was rapidly industrializing, and Southern and Eastern Europe were exporters of labor. The industrialization of the United States involved, first, the construction of a transportation infrastructure (mainly the railroads) and, second, the building of heavy industry. Both of these activities were funded by the importation of capital, through loans, from the United Kingdom, France, Germany, and Holland, and the importation of a huge new workforce, from many locations in Europe, mainly the South and East (Bankston, 2009c).

Because the new immigrants went disproportionately into the expanding North American industries, during the heaviest immigration decades they mainly settled in American cities, creating new ethnic neighborhoods. Migration did occur along network lines: people often migrated because they had friends and relatives in America and they often found work through co-ethnic ties. Within the urban ethnic enclaves, they formed ties within their groups. As the "white ethnics" created by the period's immigration came to dominate occupational fields, they engaged in "opportunity hoarding" and either attempted to steer jobs toward those within their own ethnic networks or explicitly excluded outsiders, particularly African Americans.

From the end of World War I to around 1970, the United States, having reached industrial maturity, was an exporter of goods and capital to the rest of the world, providing the structural basis for upward mobility on the part of the children and grandchildren of immigrants. From 1970 onward, though, the superpower increasingly imported goods made more cheaply in industrializing parts of the world. To the extent that it maintained its traditional domestic industries, it did so through technological efficiency, lessening demand for workers in many sectors. At the same time, it also became a financial center as both domestic profits and the dollars earned by industrializing nations abroad sought places for investment. Both the increasing technological efficiency and the expansion of the financial sector of the American economy meant that this economy became more knowledge-intensive and more capital-intensive.

As the jobs in older American industries declined, the urban areas associated with those industries also declined and central city populations, heavily made up of African Americans whose predecessors had experienced the "opportunity hoarding" of an earlier generation of workers created by immigration, found themselves in places with limited economic opportunities. Industry, however, did not disappear, nor did jobs in domestic industry go away. At the bottom end of the labor market created by the new global economy, America's consumer society created new jobs. One source of lower-level new jobs followed from the capital-intensive financial sector. Homeownership increased steadily. This was encouraged by government policy, but also by the need for investment. Especially from the 1990s until the housing crash in 2008, home loans were ever-easier to obtain. Part of the reason for this was precisely that the growing financial sector needed to find investments for domestic and foreign capital, and mortgage loans were seen as profitable investments, particularly given the growing practice of securitizing loans in new packages and marketing them. More mortgages to more people meant more homes and someone had to build those homes. Construction became a boom industry, demanding workers. Moreover, it demanded particular types of workers: those who were cheap, semi-skilled, and highly mobile and flexible.

Technological change in construction diminished the need for highly skilled workers and increased demand for the semi-skilled (Thieblot, 2002). The housing boom meant that construction work was chiefly available in building private homes, rather than public buildings. The construction industry in general is highly volatile and seasonal, requiring a flexible labor force, and this is especially true of private home construction. Other new industries also arose. During the 1970s and 1980s, for example, the American meat-processing industry became more consolidated, controlled by fewer and larger firms at just the time when skill requirements were falling in highly mechanized, large-scale meat-processing plants. The plants moved out of their old urban locations and began to look for cheaper labor. At the same time, what remained of the American textile and carpet industries also moved out of the urban centers, to Southern rural areas, and also sought cheap labor, along with technological efficiency, in order to remain competitive in a global market.

A growing service sector accompanied these changes. High consumption meant that personal services were in demand, and jobs such as those of cashiers, operating machines that automatically calculated change, were widely available. While economic opportunity had decreased in the old urban centers, people still needed to buy groceries and other materials, so that services to the relatively disadvantaged were still in demand.

While globalization created jobs in an informal, flexible sector at the bottom of the economy, the growing technological sophistication together with the expansion and centralization of financial activities also opened up positions for the highly skilled. As Ivan Light has written in his insightful discussion of immigrant networks within a globalizing context,

> globalization attracts two types of migrants to the developed core countries. A minority are skilled professionals, who earn high incomes.

The Asian Indian migrants . . . belong to this class, as do the Korean and Chinese immigrants . . . The majority, however, are poor people from the developing world, who flood into big cities in response to demand for informal sector jobs (such as nannies, gardeners, roofers, construction workers) on the part of newly wealthy households. The Mexican and Central American immigrants belong to this category. (Light, 2006: 49)

The only modifications I would make to Light's observation are that it overemphasizes the big cities at a time when immigrants are spreading out to new suburban and rural destinations, and that the new immigrant working class does not work only as employees of wealthy individuals.

Within this new global economic arrangement, it had become easier than ever to import and export people, as well as capital and goods. Reed Ueda (2007) has observed that the new processes of the world economy have reconfigured immigration. "American immigration," according to Ueda, "has occurred in a worldwide environment of rapid resource and asset flow that involves international capital, transcultural images and ideas, and technology and human capital flows. Advanced transportation and communication systems, transnational social networks, and migrant facilitators and traffickers have multiplied the possible pathways for the movement of populations into and out of the country" (pp. 25–6).

A Spanish-Speaking Working Class

People from just south of the U.S. border were geographically situated to meet the new North American demand for low-wage labor in the rapidly growing construction industry, in the new industries, and in personal services. The housing boom, stimulated by the nation's role as an international financial center, created an intense demand for construction laborers who could provide a largely seasonal and flexible labor force. By 2004, foreign-born Hispanics comprised 7 percent of the total U.S. labor force, but over 15 percent of the construction labor force. Just three years later, foreign-born Hispanics had increased to 19 percent of all workers in the American construction industry (Pew Hispanic Center, 2007). In creating demand for a construction labor force from Latin America, the global economy also contributed to the gendered character of migration and the gendered formation of immigrant networks, since construction workers are disproportionately men. At the same time, the growth of the service sector created an increase in demand for domestic workers, who are more often women, channeling immigrants along gendered tracks.

Ivan Light (2006) has argued that the sheer volume of Latino immigrants arriving at the end of the twentieth century and the beginning of the twenty-first began to saturate traditional destinations. Together with growing political animosity toward immigrants in the traditional locations, this saturation began to push immigrants out to new locations. As immigrants shifted to new locations, their network connections also shifted. Light's supply-driven account of changing immigrant migration patterns, though, must be supplemented with a critical demand-side consideration: immigrants may leave an older location because of declining opportunities, but they will only go to particular new locations if some opportunities for them exist and if they have ways of learning about those opportunities and about how to get to them.

Bridging ties between Mexican Americans and connectors in the American economy served as initial linkages to new destinations. Katharine Donato, Melissa Stainbeck, and I (Donato et al., 2005) examined the early stages of the movement of Mexican workers into oil-related construction in southwestern Louisiana. We found that recruiters with contacts near the Texas–Mexico border brought immigrant workers into a sector of the construction industry that needed a flexible labor force for an increasingly volatile economic setting. Once some workers were established in Louisiana construction, network ties among Mexican workers brought others into the activities, and the networks themselves took shape around finding these types of jobs.

The interaction between networks and economic environment can be seen in other concentrations of the growing Spanish-speaking

working class. As the poultry industry simplified its skill requirements and moved out of urban to rural areas, Gainesville, in
northern Georgia, became known as the "Poultry Capital of the
World," processing chicken meat for shipping to national and
international markets. The first Mexican workers began arriving
in northern Georgia in the 1970s, establishing a basis for network
support and communication for future arrivals. In social capital
terms, being part of a Mexican immigrant network became an
asset that could be used to obtain work in the poultry industry.
Consequently, as immigrants made use of their network assets
their numbers began to rise rapidly in the 1980s (Kaushal et al.,
2008; Guthey, 2001).

Their networks also served to move across industries, following
the same pattern of some immigrant workers establishing a presence in a setting amenable to immigrant labor, and then bringing in
others along their lines of contact. Textile and carpet manufacturing businesses, drawn by the competitive advantages of the South's
lower wages, had relocated from the Northeast to the South. The
town of Dalton, Georgia, emerged as a center of this industry,
producing 80 percent of all the carpets in the United States by
the late 1990s. Mexican workers who had come to work in north
Georgia's poultry industry in the mid-1980s found other regional
opportunities, including the carpet industry, through their links
with co-ethnics. Other Mexican immigrants, pushed further north
by a slowdown in the Texas building industry, as well as by the
longer-term orientation created by American immigration policy,
came to the area. Perceptions of a labor shortage among carpet
manufacturing employers in this small town combined with the
relatively low wages that Mexican immigrants would accept made
the new arrivals attractive to employers, reinforcing the network
channels, and Mexicans moved into the industry on a large scale
during the 1990s (Hernández-León and Zúñiga, 2003; 2006).

Middleman Minority Networks and Professional Migrants

America's shifting role within the global economy after 1970
created new industries that created a new working class, but it

also produced a decline in many of the old industries, especially in urban areas, as traditional heavy industries moved to other parts of the world. The nation's central cities experienced heavy unemployment, mainly among the now largely urban African American population.

Small businesses in central city areas had long been the province of ethnic minority merchants, and the gradual movement of these merchants to more suburban locations contributed to opening up positions for entrepreneurs. The movement of Koreans into these positions was more than ethnic succession, though. In a study of the growth of immigrant Korean entrepreneurship in Chicago, In-Jin Yoon (1995) wrote "faced with a rising crime rate, decreasing profitability, and surrounded by blacks who were hostile to white businesses, white business owners had a strong desire to move to another location. Thus, before Korean immigrants entered black areas to open their businesses, the combination of changing ethnic composition and civil disorder left a vacancy in business opportunities in black areas" (p. 327).

Initially, the Korean merchants that In-Jin Yoon has studied specialized in inexpensive wigs in response to fashions in the relatively low-income black communities they served. The ties of these merchants to manufacturers abroad assisted them in producing for this market. However, Koreans also moved into small groceries and other types of stores in majority black urban communities. Eventually, the financial capital some accumulated enabled them to shift to more profitable forms of entrepreneurship, such as the real estate market in Los Angeles that Ivan Light (2006) has examined.

The migration of Koreans was often network-driven. Coming from a more distant location than Mexicans, though, and more dependent on legal avenues of migration, the Korean networks worked in different ways. Whereas those from south of the border would show up in places where ethnic communities had been established and seek information and help from the members of those communities, Korean connections determined the very ability to move. Therefore, as Koreans moved into the new country, they tended to build solid forms of cooperation with each other in specific places, rather than traveling around the country looking for jobs. Moreover, while Korean immigration did increase sharply beginning in the 1980s, this was always a much smaller group than that of the Spanish-speaking workers. The combination of relatively small group size, high network interdependence, and human capital in the form of entrepreneurial skills encouraged the shaping of Korean American networks around the investment-oriented positions in the interstices of the American economy. While middleman minority entrepreneurship continued to be a common occupational location for Korean immigrants, though, the growing international links between the United States and Korea, combined with the increase in demand for professionals, made immigration from Korea in socioeconomically advantaged positions increasingly common.

By the early 2000s, Korean immigrants entering under the employment preference category began to outnumber those entering under the family reunification categories, as can be seen in the Department of Homeland Security's *Yearbook of Immigration Statistics* over the years. U.S. Census data show that self-employment among relatively recent Korean immigrants peaked in 1990, and then began to decrease, although it remained a common form of economic activity. By contrast, though, employment in managerial and professional specialty occupations grew steadily over the years, so that by the time of the 2007–11 five-year American Community Survey, a majority of comparatively new (10 years in the U.S. or under) employed Korean immigrants were working as managers and professionals (Ruggles et al., 2010).

The dual concentrations of Koreans, in self-employment and in professional employment, had important network implications. The ethnic organizations, especially churches, that brought Koreans together in the United States consisted of people who had useful information to communicate, and who could promote upward mobility for younger people.

Vietnamese: Mixed Services, Labor, and Ethnic Economies

Immigrant groups produced by refugee flows are in some ways unique. First, they are produced by the political side of the global environment, rather than the economic side. Second, as a corollary, refugee movements and resettlements have a degree of active governmental involvement missing in other forms of immigration.

Despite the uniqueness of refugee migration, the social networks of refugee groups have taken shape within the social and economic setting determined by global contexts. In the case of the Vietnamese, and other Southeast Asian refugee groups, for example, government-directed resettlement initially attempted to spread new arrivals widely across the nation. However, secondary migration, utilizing ethnic networks with family relations at the core, created ethnic clusters around the country. Moreover, these clusters tended to locate in suburban areas within a suburbanizing society, following a pattern found among contemporary non-immigrant groups. Although the Vietnamese (and other Southeast Asians) did settle in large metropolitan areas, most notably in southern California, they located mainly in the lower-income parts of the suburban rings of older cities and in newer post-automobile metropolitan areas that had minimal identifiable central cities.

In a comparison of the employment distributions of Vietnamese, Koreans, and Chinese in 1980 individual-level Census data, Min Zhou and I found that the Vietnamese were spread across a range of industries and showed relatively little self-employment at that time (Zhou and Bankston, 1992). Just as ethnic networks created residential communities through secondary migration, though, those networks also shifted economic activities during the 1980s. For example, in our examination of Vietnamese employment in Louisiana, Min Zhou and I found that from the 1980 Census to the 1990 Census, the state's Vietnamese had largely moved out of manufacturing jobs and into fishing and food-related industries, and that self-employment in fishing, small groceries, and eating and drinking establishments had increased sharply (Bankston and Zhou, 1996). Unlike groceries and restaurants, work in fishing is regional in character, concentrated as it is along the coasts. Still, the means by which the Vietnamese became concentrated in this industry are illustrative of broader network processes. Our Vietnamese informants told us that they went into fishing because of a lack of opportunities in the wider economy. "Like agriculture, another extractive industry that employs a disproportionate share of minority workers," we reported, "the fishing industry has a demand for low wage manual labor" (Bankston and Zhou, 1996: 48). Thus, the Vietnamese in fishing represented one tendency within the new American globalized work setting: a low-wage immigrant labor force. This tendency could be seen elsewhere, such as in the seafood processing industries that emerged all along the Gulf Coast (Bankston, 2012b).

In some respects, then, the Vietnamese fit into the late twentieth- and early twenty-first-century American setting as Latinos did, by becoming part of the nation's new internationalized working class. However, the smaller size of the Vietnamese population, compared to the Spanish speakers, and the reconcentration of the Vietnamese into fairly dense ethnic clusters around the nation also made possible some upward mobility that resembled the more entrepreneurial ethnic groups. In our study of the Vietnamese in fishing, our informants reported that they had been able to purchase fishing boats by pooling incomes and assisting each other (Bankston and Zhou, 1996). The same network assets that enabled them to buy boats (and hire other Vietnamese to work on the boats) also enabled them to go into other businesses, notably in the service sector, at the interstices of the contemporary American economy.

Within the personal-service-oriented American consumer economy, the Vietnamese beauty and nail salon became almost a stereotypical occupation. Indeed, the 2010 five-year American Community Survey of the Census Bureau shows that "hairdressers and beauticians" made up over 13 percent of all Vietnamese Americans in the labor force, more than any other occupational concentration. The most common industries were miscellaneous personal services, eating and drinking places, electrical machinery, and beauty shops, which together employed over one-fifth of all Vietnamese workers in the United States (Ruggles et al., 2010).

The regathering of Vietnamese into communities in the United States enabled them to use their network connections to move into small-scale entrepreneurial activities. Just as these networks formed within the context of their resettlement in the new country, though, these networks could only give them access to positions available. Some became part of the internationalized working class, but others entered lower-level service jobs. Still others were able to follow the middleman minority path of immigrant retailers serving minority customers. Thus, when the Vietnamese were able to use ethnic ties to raise funds, these funds sometimes went into opening small corner grocery stores in locations that were underserved by the big chains. Even more often, though, the funds went into opening service-oriented businesses such as ethnic restaurants, especially Vietnamese noodle places, and beauty or nail shops. In collaborating to raise funds or hiring co-ethnics or recruiting family members to work in businesses, the Vietnamese were organizing their networks around these types of positions.

Filipinos: Professional Immigrants to an Aging Developed Nation

The United States and the Philippines clearly have a long and complicated history of relations with each other. The high rate of spousal migration from the Philippines, American-style educational credentials, and generally sophisticated language skills can all be traced to American influence in the island nation. The extensive transnational connections between Filipinos and Filipino Americans also testify to extensive two-way linkages across the ocean. Nevertheless, the story of Filipino American immigration in general and of Filipino American social networks in particular is also part of a broader story about globalization.

The American takeover of the Philippines initiated the U.S. rise as an international power. By about 1970, the time at which Filipino migration increased sharply, the place of the United States on the world scene had shifted to that of a relatively post-industrial, highly developed, consumer economy. Although it continued to be one of the world's most productive nations, its level of consumption meant that it brought in goods, capital, and labor from all over the world, while it outsourced many of its heavy industry activities. One of the most notable characteristics of highly developed nations is that they tend to be aging nations, and this greatly intensifies the demand for medical care.

Because of their skill levels, Filipinos in the United States tend to be found in the knowledge-intensive sectors of the cheap labor–service–knowledge structure created by the American place in the global economy, with heavy representations in occupations such as accountants, engineers, and teachers. More than anywhere else, though, those Filipino immigrants who are not marriage migrants (and many who are) tend to be located in medical occupations: "about 13% of Filipino Americans in 2000 were physicians, surgeons, nurses, or medical technicians . . . and one out of every six to seven immigrant Filipino women was a nurse" (Bankston, 2006: 191). To point out the broader importance of the Filipino example for immigrant groups in general, this same pattern of disproportionately professional employment with a strong specialization in medical occupations is characteristic of others, most notably the Asian Indians, who share with Filipinos English-language skills rooted in colonial history and educational credentials that are generally readily transferable. In addition, the demand for nurses reinforced the central role of gender in Filipino immigration and in Filipino immigrant social networks.

The type of immigration channeled to the United States from the Philippines by the economic setting created by globalization had notable consequences for network structure and for the kinds of assets transmitted along network lines. On the one hand, Filipino American immigrant networks are pathways for family-based immigration, information transfer, and identity support. On the other, in their jobs and even in their marriage partners Filipino Americans are heavily embedded in mainstream American society.

To answer the question of how one can have both immigrant networks and individual incorporation in a host society, one should reflect that modern life takes place on many different stages. Workplaces, families, and friendship groups can be separate and distinct spheres. The Asian Indian physician, for example, may work in a hospital or clinic with members of other ethnic groups and belong to a variety of non-Indian professional organizations, while maintaining mostly Asian Indian personal friends and going home to an Asian Indian family. Filipino American immigrants offer a more subtle version of the same phenomenon:

ethnic networks among individuals who also maintain extensive and even intimate bridging ties with people outside the ethnic group. These networks are not reducible to cultural heritage, but result from the setting of modern Filipino American immigrants in the larger contexts of international relations and the positions of nations in the modern world.

In this general view of networks within and across nations, I have concentrated on the importance of contexts of migrations: contexts of exit and reception, and the context of how globalization shapes immigration and the positions of different immigrant groups within nations. Having looked at the contexts that shape immigrant networks, I will proceed in Chapters 4 through 6 to examine families, communities, and organizations as immigrant network structures.

4

Family Ties

From a network perspective, the family can be understood as a pattern of linkages among individuals. This view of the family was at the heart of James S. Coleman's description of social capital (1990), which attributed social assets to the way in which binding ties are arranged among family members, and to how bridging ties connect families to external institutions. Coleman concentrated on nuclear families and on their consequences for the human capital attainment of children, but similar and related ideas about family-based connections can easily be expanded to apply to extended family relationships and to connections among adults. To the extent that family is a basis for ties among adults, those ties can constrain individuals to motivate cooperation and sharing of resources and information and enable them to make use of the assistance of other family members. The constraining and enabling produced by family relations depend on norms about the obligations of relatives, but also on network closure and density of interconnections: a set of highly transitive bounded connections among relatives can reinforce individuals' obligations to each other. The importance of these connections depends on available alternatives. People who can easily break with all of their family members or assign family to a secondary place in their lives are less influenced by kin groups than those who need to rely on their relatives.

American immigration law tends to heighten the functional importance of family linkages among transnational ties. Figure

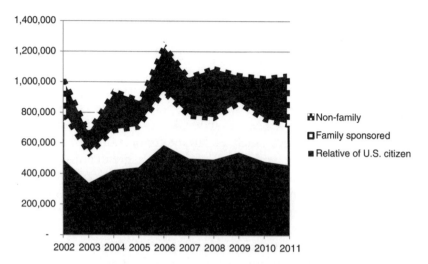

Figure 4.1 Numbers of Legal Permanent Residents Admitted to the United States as Immediate Relatives of Citizens, as Family-Sponsored Immigrants, and in Non-Family Categories, 2002–11

Source: United States Department of Homeland Security, 2012: table 6.

4.1 shows numbers of people admitted to the United States as permanent residents who were immediate relatives of U.S. citizens, family-sponsored immigrants, and those admitted under all other preference categories. Most legal migration has taken place along family lines. These numbers, moreover, actually underestimate the part played by family connections. Immigrants admitted under the employment preference category can and do sponsor family members or become citizens and bring in members of their immediate family.

Undocumented immigrants also use family connections for migration. Those in a country without legal recognition have greater need of links with people they can trust. An undocumented immigrant showing up in a strange North American city normally can place greater confidence in a relative, especially a close relative, than almost anyone else. As I will discuss in more detail, though, undocumented migrants are often likely to follow the information provided by weak ties to find jobs in new locations, only later bringing families after them. This is also true regardless of documentation for immigrants who follow the common undocumented pattern of seeking job opportunities available to members of the new working class.

Differences in the migration functions of kinship networks suggest that the weak ties–strong ties issue can be complicated. Granovetter (1973) argued that weak ties are frequently more useful than strong ties (such as family connections) because the former extend more widely and bring in a greater diversity of information. However, as I will discuss in greater detail in Chapter 7, it appears that the immigrants who rely most heavily on weak ties are those finding positions at the bottom of the contemporary American class structure.

The fact that the functions of kinship networks vary depending on contextual setting draws attention to variations in the extent to which groups are able to maintain and make use of these sorts of networks, and in the assets provided by family members. Despite the importance of kin for migration, moving from one place to another can in many situations weaken social networks and disrupt family ties. When Wierzbicki (2004) examined kinship ties in Los Angeles, she suggested that migrants should have fewer family connections precisely because they would have left family members behind, while native-born residents with the least mobility would have the greatest number of family ties. This was indeed what she found. "Immigrants and internal migrants," she reported, "find themselves in similar situations of having fewer kin available in the area than those who grew up in Los Angeles" (p. 75). However, apart from this migration effect, she also found that ethnic minorities (African Americans, Hispanics, and Asians) had fewer overall social ties than non-Hispanic whites, and that ethnic minorities and lower-income people were more likely to report ties chiefly or exclusively with family members than non-Hispanic whites or more economically advantaged individuals. The family ties of ethnic minorities and the disadvantaged, in addition, provided relatively few avenues for upward mobility because family members had access to limited resources and information. So immigrants, as newcomers, had relatively small networks in general. They tended to be connected mainly to family members, but there were few of these family members available. Although the strong bonds of kin group members could help them out with crises and provide essential support, these were not enabling ties in the sense of enabling opportunities for improved lives.

This description of immigrant family networks is a good one, and its summary findings provide an excellent basis for thinking about the topic, but I suggest that the ways that family networks function among immigrants is more complicated and varied than this. One consideration is that in many circumstances immigrants may have fewer kin ties, but that the strength of the kin tie may be more intense than it is for non-immigrants precisely because of the lack of alternatives. A second consideration is that because kinship is a means of migration, in some settings family may be especially important as a means of reconstituting community in the new homeland. A third is that migration may create family connections by giving new functional importance to kin relations that may have been only passively recognized prior to migration. A fourth is that for some groups either migration along family lines or secondary migration may concentrate family members, creating family-based communities with multiple, interlinking kinship ties. A fifth is that the assets possessed by family members vary from one immigrant group to another. Finally, some immigrant groups may be able to combine family networks with extensive bridging ties, with consequences for social assets. In order to illustrate these variations among immigrant family networks, I turn now to specific groups, concentrating on the four major groups examined in Chapter 3.

Families Across the Border

Research on Mexican immigrant networks suggests that immigration may begin on the basis of relatively weak ties, but that as immigrants establish a greater presence in locations on the North American side of the border, kinship networks become more important as transnational ties. Flores-Yeffal and Aysa-Lastra

(2011) found that people from the same place of origin in Mexico, or *paisanos*, were especially important at the beginning of a migratory flow from a location. As more migrants from a location settled, though, friends and family played a greater part. These authors interpreted these differences in terms of Granovetter's distinction between strong and weak ties, suggesting that the utility of different types of ties depended on the situation. As immigrants from the southern side of the border spread out into new settlement destinations, they tend to rely on their regional contacts who can communicate information about unfamiliar places. However, as settlement becomes denser, strong ties such as kinship ties become important as support networks.

This pattern immediately offers somewhat of a contrast with immigration to the United States in general, especially legal migration, which tends to begin on the basis of family ties. Some of the best insights into the migration process in recent years have come from the work of Rubén Hernández-León and Victor Zúñiga, whose extensive fieldwork enabled them to describe the emergence of a Mexican immigrant settlement in Georgia in response to labor demand in a new carpet-making industry. Hernández-León and Zúñiga (2000) found that early arrivals tended to be single men, who had heard about the availability of jobs in Georgia from co-ethnic acquaintances. Notably, many of these men were secondary migrants from the traditional Hispanic labor immigrant region of the Southwest. They were moving to new parts of the United States, looking for jobs in construction and in developing industries such as meat-packing and carpet manufacture. Women and children followed the men, sometimes from the Southwest but also sometimes directly from Mexico.

This process of initial trailblazers, followed by families and the reconstitution of communities, can be found across a variety of immigrant groups and it has been described as a generalizable series of stages (Massey et al., 1994). However, Mexican (and Central American) immigrants stand out for three reasons. First, in recent history "trailblazing" has played an especially large part in migration due to the highly mobile character of Mexican migration as a response to changes in American labor demand. Second, their situation as inhabitants of the same land mass as North America has enabled them to move across the border more readily and, once across the border, to move to new locations with more tenuous networks. Third, because initially undocumented migration (despite the amnesties following the Immigration Reform and Control Act (IRCA) of 1986) has such a large part in the movement across the Mexican–U.S. border, the first-stage migration has not been channeled through the family-oriented preference categories.

Clearly, among Mexican immigrants family reunification does take place. Hernández-León and Zúñiga (2000) remarked that what they saw happening in Georgia "is not atypical and reflects the experience of traditional receiving areas such as Houston, Chicago, and Los Angeles" (p. 62). The amnesty of undocumented immigrants under the IRCA provisions created kin nuclei and created wider settlements. Once family members followed the trailblazers, dual earner households became common, suggesting that information flows through kinship connections became ways to find working-class jobs later in the immigration process.

Looking at another emerging immigrant settlement, in New Orleans following Hurricane Katrina, several of my co-authors and I found similar developments (Donato et al., 2010). There, also, a new industry brought in job seekers from Mexico and Central America. Hurricane reconstruction work attracted Latin American migrants to the area, many of whom were secondary migrants, already working in construction and related industries in other parts of the United States. As in the Georgia example, these initial arrivals were disproportionately men, drawn either by recruiters or by word of mouth from co-ethnic associates in the same line of work, emphasizing once again the gendered nature of Mexican migration (see Donato and Patterson, 2004). Families began to follow these men within two years of the arrival of the Latin American workforce. Once families had arrived, more complex immigrant communities developed, with businesses specializing in sending remittances and ethnically oriented stores and restaurants. While this did create some limited upward mobility for the entrepreneurs who opened those businesses, most of the available jobs for the immigrants continued to be in that new working class of laborers and semi-skilled construction and personal services.

The common identifiable migration process for Latin Americans, then, consists of the American economic structure opening up jobs with relatively low socioeconomic status, migration across the border and secondary migration primarily on the basis of information about those jobs through weak ties, family members following single workers, and the development of ethnic communities oriented toward those new working-class positions with limited upward mobility. The evidence indicates, though, that high geographic mobility continues to characterize these immigrant settlements. In my interviews with teachers in schools located in the suburban neighborhoods outside of the city of New Orleans, where the immigrants have concentrated, the teachers have repeatedly said that one of their greatest pedagogical challenges is the nomadic tendency of their Latin American students. The teachers say that they have new students constantly arriving. But they also insist that students are constantly leaving the district and that students tell the teachers they will be leaving because their families are following their fathers to still other locations because of the quest for work.

While weak ties may be important for people from Latin America in the quest for the working-class jobs available in North America, though, families do remain relevant to the migration process. In fact, migration may redefine family to place greater emphasis on extended family ties. Studying southern California, Chávez (1985; 1990) found that Mexican immigrants often lived in extended family households in the early years of migration, but that they tended to shift to nuclear families as they remained longer. Moreover, long-established migration areas, especially along the border, tend to develop sending and receiving kinship networks (Bastida, 2001). Georgia has developed elaborate kinship networks for receiving and supporting immigrants (Hernández-León and Zúñiga, 2000).

So non-family weak ties play a greater part in the early stages of migration to new locations and in movement to more distant locations. As settlement is established, family networks become more important, and these networks frequently come to include more extended kin. With long settlement, the extended kin networks become less prevalent and families are inclined to contract to nuclear form. However, the new destinations phenomenon – that is, the fact that opportunities at the bottom of the American labor market are continually pulling Latin American immigrants to new places – means that this cycle is continually ongoing.

In terms of how family social capital translates into financial capital, the location of most Latin American families in the larger stratification system means that the families offer support systems for maintenance rather than for upward mobility. Without access to much financial capital, family networks relatively rarely (compared with many other immigrant groups) become sources of sufficient monetary accumulation to invest in small businesses. Because expectations are built on experiences that have been channeled by their histories as members of the cross-border working class, Latin American immigrants reasonably understand their kin networks as means of basic support, rather than as mechanisms for collaborating in upward mobility. The trend toward nuclear families among long-staying immigrants appears to be largely a consequence of this basic support function of extended kinship networks, rather than of purely cultural preferences. Once immigrants have been in a place long enough that they no longer require essential support, the extended kinship networks lose their functional importance.

Using family social capital to produce human capital through the U.S. school system is similarly problematic. Latin American immigrant families do perceive schooling as a route to upward mobility for their children, and immigrant Latin American children frequently do better in American schools than native-born children of Latin American heritage (see Chapter 8). Nevertheless, Latin American students in general have fairly low rates of academic achievement and attainment and high dropout rates. Much of this can be attributed to the socioeconomic context. The status of Mexicans and Central Americans as a large new working class tends to settle them in highly segregated neighborhoods. For children in immigrant families, in particular, the high geographic mobility means that their families may frequently move from one segregated neighborhood to another. Kin networks that serve mainly to provide basic support and to convey information about job opportunities at the margins of the economy do not offer the tightly interlocking sets of connections that will control and direct young people toward advancing through the school system. (On the interactions between networks and the stratification system in producing school outcomes, see Stanton-Salazar, 2001.)

Here, I want to emphasize that whether social ties provide support for maintenance or control and direction is a matter of degree, not a dichotomy. One should not see Latino kin networks as lacking the capacity for promoting upward mobility, but as tending toward the maintenance side of the maintenance–upward mobility continuum. In addition, if we consider networks as information channels, problems such as undocumented status can limit opportunities for employment by family members, thereby limiting information available through kin.

Korean Family Networks and Mobility Strategies

In Chapter 3, I pointed out that although Korean immigrants historically have tended to concentrate in small-scale entrepreneurship, this is a strategy rather than a goal. Koreans employ social capital, notably family social capital, to generate the financial capital for self-employment. The self-employment, in turn, can generate social capital for investment in the human capital of the second generation because businesses become bases for intergenerational connections among parents and children.

Immigrants from Korea to the United States fit into a socioeconomic context that contrasts radically with that of Latin Americans. A substantial number of the Koreans today arrive to take up professional occupations, a fact that is reflected in the relatively high proportion of new legal permanent residents from Korea admitted in recent years under the job preference category (55 percent in 2011, 52 percent in 2010, 55 percent in 2009, according to the *Yearbook of Immigration Statistics* (United States Department of Homeland Security, 2012), while nearly all others were admitted under family-sponsored preferences or as immediate relatives of U.S. citizens. This predominance of professional immigrants is a recent phenomenon, though. As recently as the 1990s, family-based migration was still the norm for arrivals from Korea. The two family categories accounted for 71 percent of admissions from Korea in 1999, 66 percent in 1998, and 66 percent in 1997. This family-based migration has historically, since 1965, been the main avenue for Korean migration, which has over the years been mainly a matter of chain migration along family network lines (Yoo, 2000).

Evidence indicates that adaptation after migration tends to place an additional emphasis on kin relations, so that family networks are often more important for Korean immigrants than family connections are for people living in Korea. Looking at Korean immigrant families in Atlanta, Pyong Gap Min (1984) found that kin assistance was the most important source of help not only for immigrant orientation, but also for financial and other settlements. Immigration, Min concluded, enhances family ties.

While professional immigrants have found jobs in the mainstream sector, the family-based migrants, logically, have made up the largest portion of those in the small-scale entrepreneurship that has become so closely associated with Korean Americans that it is an ethnic stereotype. Wider social networks are critical as channels of information about opportunities for opening businesses and can provide financial assistance, but loans from families or relatives appear to be the most common capital source after personal savings. In a study of Korean small businesses in Atlanta, Yoo (2000: 359) finds "a clear tendency of heavy reliance on family networks (i.e. loans from family or relatives) for capital mobilization other than personal savings, which indicates that family networks are a crucial financial resource."

The businesses established by Koreans in the United States are usually family businesses. Although extended family members may provide financial and other kinds of support in establishing businesses, the day-to-day work of running the business falls on the nuclear family. Kim (2006) found that although Korean immigrant entrepreneurs did not demand as much unpaid labor from their children as immigrant entrepreneurs elsewhere in the world, it was the norm for children to contribute to the family businesses, working with their parents.

Despite the fact that these are family businesses, entrepreneurial Korean immigrants most often do not want their children to follow them into self-employment. Instead, they want their children to obtain educational credentials that will make it possible for the children to enter professional occupations in the United States. The background of schooling among immigrant parents may not be immediately relevant to finding commensurate positions for the parents, but this schooling does enable them to communicate to their children the importance of formal education and the habits that will enable the children to be successful in school. "Korean immigrant professionals," Dae Young Kim remarks (2006: 951), "come equipped with class advantage that assists their children to succeed in education and attain professional occupations."

This class advantage of immigrant parents is conveyed primarily within sets of family relations. Eunjung Kim (2002) has noted that Korean immigrant parents tend to show relatively low levels of school-based involvement in their children's lives. This is at odds with the model of intergenerational closure described by James Coleman, which portrays social capital as involving transitive connections among parents and teachers, as well as other adults. However, Kim observes that Korean parents also show high levels of home-based involvement.

The reluctance of parents to become involved with teachers or in school organizations is understandable, given the language barrier and work demands on the time of parents. To fully understand the home-based involvement, and how this can be seen as social capital generating human capital, though, we should reflect that for the many entrepreneurial Korean immigrants home and business are closely interconnected. Although Kim (2006) argued that family businesses can constrain the opportunities of the Korean American second generation, Kim also observed precisely how the interconnections within Korean entrepreneurial families could translate into academic success:

> manageable amounts of helping out limited children's time spent on socializing, thereby increasing parental supervision and indirectly affecting academic performance. An empathetic understanding of parental struggles as immigrant entrepreneurs, including feelings of obligations to help out in the family business, pulled the second generation to parental and community norms toward education, work, and family enterprise ... Embracing the rhetoric of parental sacrifice and family business success for children's education pushed the second generation to help out and do well in school. (Kim, 2006: 949)

For the Koreans who emphasized the entrepreneurial strategy, small, family-based businesses provided places for establishing intergenerational closure, a network characteristic commonly identified as a form of social capital. Family networks, then, were first a means of moving to the United States through chain migration, then a source of financial capital for establishing businesses, which, in turn, became the basis for nuclear family relationships. The professional immigrants, of course, could pass their class advantages on to their children. These included their own high levels of schooling and their relatively privileged positions in American society.

Refugees: Extended Families for Relocation and Support

As Min Zhou and I (1998) noted, much of the history of Vietnamese settlement in the United States can be seen as a process of family fragmentation, reconstruction, and strategic extension of kinship relations. Vietnamese refugees often arrived in fragments of nuclear or extended families because individuals were often unable to flee their original homeland with all family members. The breaking up of families placed stress on both adults and children, and this has been one of the sources of problems for Vietnamese Americans over the years.

Once they had resettled in the U.S., though, both sentiment and the need for family network support led to intense efforts by individuals to reunify and extend family connections. The extensive secondary migration that contributed greatly to the creation of Vietnamese American ethnic communities took place largely along the lines of internal family chain migration. As newcomers to a strange country, the Vietnamese needed to find people who could offer familiarity and who could help with psychological and economic adjustment. In order to find the social circles that could serve these purposes, family boundaries were often redefined to bring distant relatives or adoptive relations who would have been marginal members of families in Vietnam into the active set of kin relations in the United States (Hein, 1995; Kibria, 1993). In reconstructed families, members shared common experiences of flight and relocation and developed a sense of collective strength in coping, giving rise to new mechanisms in re-establishing social ties and networks of support, such as cooperative kinship-based economic practices (Hitchcox, 1988; Kibria, 1993).

The reconstructed, extended families formed by members of refugee groups to adapt to life in an unaccustomed land became critical sources of financial capital. Among the Vietnamese shrimpers that Min Zhou and I interviewed in the New Orleans area, accumulating funds and making or enabling loans among relatives became a primary way of making the purchase of shrimp boats possible. Elsewhere in the United States, as well as in that New Orleans community, families re-established and broadened for the sake of resettlement became springboards to business activities. One illustration of this can be drawn from the Vietnamese settlement in Houston.

After the fall of Saigon, Houston resident Vican Tan initially resettled in Paris, where he studied and held part-time dishwashing and busboy jobs. In 1982, though, he moved to Houston to reunite with his parents and five sisters. His parents helped him secure a loan to open a grocery store catering to Vietnamese and other shoppers. All of his family members worked with him in the business, which became the Viet Hoa International Foods Supermarket, with customers from a wide range of ethnic backgrounds. While in school, his teenaged sons helped in this expansion by doing paperwork and stocking shelves (Patel, 2005).

Within the hairdressing and beautician occupational category that was the single greatest concentration of Vietnamese in the U.S. labor force, manicures and pedicures have been the Vietnamese specialization. Again, this specialization must be seen as an opportunity made possible by the expansion of demand for personal services in the American economy. Answering the question of how the Vietnamese moved into this specialization, though, entails examining interpersonal connections within families looking for opportunities within underserved markets. In somewhat the same manner that Korean wig merchants found relatively little competition in selling wigs to the African American market or opening stores in neighborhoods neglected by the national chains, the new Vietnamese population found relatively few competitors and many clients for manicure and pedicure services. Once again, an anecdote may help illustrate the role of family networks within this specialization.

Binh Nguyen, founder and president of the Vietnamese American Chamber of Commerce in the Washington, D.C., area, owns a number of businesses, but the foundation of his success is the academy he owns in Virginia that trains Vietnamese nail technicians. His relatives moved into the manicure business after arriving in California in the early 1980s, and they brought Mr. Nguyen's mother into the business. She, in turn, insisted that he learn to do nails. When California became too crowded with manicurists, the family re-established itself in the Washington area (Lazo, 2012).

Whatever the future involvement of the Vietnamese in family businesses will be, it has become clear that the reconstructed, extended families of former refugees do furnish social capital to contribute to school success. Vietnamese immigrant parents, like Korean parents, generally do not maintain close ties with teachers and school officials, in part because of language problems (Zhou and Bankston, 2000). The extended family linkages, however, create tight interpersonal networks around young people, providing direction and control. These extended family linkages, produced by the strangeness of American society for newly arrived refugees, also connect families to communities, surrounding children with a web of adult social contacts.

Outward Assimilation and Immigrant Family Networks: The Filipino Example

In 2011, 87 percent of people born in the Philippines admitted to the U.S. as legal permanent residents entered under the two categories of "immediate relatives of U.S." citizens and "family-sponsored immigrants," while a little less than 65 percent of immigrants from all countries came in under these two categories. Moreover, 51 percent of Filipinos arrived through the single category of immediate relatives of citizens, which refers chiefly to spouses and children, compared to 43 percent of all immigrants (U.S. Department of Homeland Security, 2012).

Family connections are the primary avenues for legal migration for people from most backgrounds. However, these are even more important for Filipino immigrants, as are immediate links to U.S. citizens. Because family migration is common and migration by marriage is a main route for several groups (Hidalgo and Bankston, 2008; 2010; 2011), we can take the Filipino case as one that highlights certain types of family migration and immigrant adaptation.

According to the five-year American Community Survey of 2007–11 (Ruggles et al., 2010), about one-fourth of all married immigrants from the Philippines had a spouse who had been born in the United States. One-third of married female Filipino immigrants had an American-born spouse. More than one out of every five currently married immigrants from the Philippines had a spouse of another detailed race. Most of these spouses (19 percent) were listed as "white." Among married women immigrants, 28 percent had white spouses and another 3 percent had African American spouses. Altogether, 36 percent of currently married Filipino immigrant women had spouses who were not Filipinos. It is not possible to determine from these statistics how many of those had entered through marriage migration and how many had married after arrival. This, however, represents a remarkably high level of out-marriage for immigrants.

The Census data provide no information about the former spouses of the one-quarter of Filipino immigrants whose spouses were not present in households or who were divorced, separated, or widowed. However, since the marriage patterns have been fairly consistent over decades (Bankston, 2006), we can assume that the racial distribution of former marriage partners is similar to that of current marriage partners. This would mean that approximately one-fourth of all Filipino immigrant women in the United States, including single women, have or have had a white or African American husband and about 29 percent of all Filipino immigrant women are currently or were formerly married to someone who was not a Filipino. It would mean that among all immigrant Filipino women of all marital statuses, including single, over one-fourth are spouses or former spouses of U.S. natives. In addition, most immigrants from the Philippines are women (over 59 percent in the 2007–11 period).

In short, women married to native-born Americans or to others who were not of Filipino ancestry constitute a huge part of the immigrant population from that country. This is a pattern found in other groups, as well, most notably in immigrants from Thailand (Hidalgo and Bankston, 2011). The pattern has implications for immigrant social networks and for the kinds of resources those networks produce.

There is a sense in which intermarriage clearly disintegrates identifiable sets of social ties among the descendants of immigrants. The children and grandchildren of Filipino or Thai parents and parents from other backgrounds will be unlikely to maintain extensive ethnically based social ties. In the short run, though, immigrant networks do play a critical, if sometimes "backstage," part in the lives of out-married Filipinos and members of other groups.

Out-married Filipino immigrants, most of whom are wives, maintain two overlapping sets of ethnic social circles. The first are those of cross-national ties with family members in the Philippines. The second are those of ties with other Filipinos in the United

States. At the center of the second circle are sets of connections among the women, although these also connect to other co-ethnics and act as unique kinds of bridging ties.

Post-1965 immigration law allows spouses, unmarried minor children, and parents of U.S. citizens to enter the country without the numerical restrictions that govern other immigrants, including family-sponsored immigrants. When a citizen of the Philippines marries an American citizen, the former is almost guaranteed acceptance as a legal permanent resident. After five years, the immigrant can become an American citizen and then bring petition for her parents or minor children by a previous marriage to immigrate outside of numerical restrictions. Even as a legal permanent resident, the immigrant can petition for family members to arrive within the quotas.

In a 1986 study of patterns of Philippine migration, De Jong, Root, and Abad found that between 1971 and 1984 the numbers of people migrating from the Philippines to the United States under the unrestricted category of immediate family members increased by two and a half times, so that by 1984 a majority (53 percent) of Filipino arrivals were unrestricted immediate family members. Family-sponsored immigrants had doubled during this period. In interviewing immigrants, De Jong et al. found that the primary way in which people in the Philippines learned about immigration procedures was through family members, most often immediate family members, in the United States.

Since the mid-1980s, Filipino immigration has increased sharply, by all the evidence as a consequence of those same family mechanisms (Bankston, 2006). It is difficult to calculate just how much of this growth can ultimately be traced to the high rate of out-marriage by Filipino women in the United States, but both logic and my own informal interviews with Filipino Americans indicate that much if not most of this migration is indirectly or directly a consequence of marriage.

Filipino wives' circles (that is, informal groups of out-married women) play an important part in maintaining immigrant networks within the United States among individuals who by many measures are highly integrated into the country's mainstream.

When two Filipino immigrants make contact, one will most often introduce the new acquaintance to other Filipinos in the area. This may occur casually. It is extremely common, for example, for immigrants to introduce themselves to strangers they hear speaking Tagalog, Visayan, or Ilocano in a public place and for the two to exchange contact information. Anecdotally, this happens much more often among women than among men, although this observation could bear more systematic investigation, particularly given the fact that Filipino women in the United States outnumber the men. The two normally exchange information about other Filipinos in an area, and chains of introductions result in national-origin friendship and support groups, maintained by dinners, parties, and other sorts of get-togethers.

The informal and person-to-person ties that make up much of Filipino networks have led Filipinos in the United States to be characterized by some as an "invisible ethnic community" (see, for example, Tyner, 2007). This invisibility may be exaggerated because there are formal organizations of Filipinos in the United States and there are some residential concentrations. However, webs of informal relationships, formed on the basis of immigrant ethnicity, are arguably central to this ethnic community, and these relationships do often lack immediate visibility.

This kind of network clearly has more the characteristics of the support group than of the closed, tightly bounded set of ties scholars normally think of when they discuss social capital. It co-exists with extensive bridging ties to the larger society and generally occupies only part of its participants' lives. As sources of social assets, informal immigrant networks primarily provide psycho-social support and convey information. This may be information about the doings of other group members, but it can also be practical information, concerning, for example, jobs and housing. The kinds of networks typified by Filipino immigrants tend not to have extensive consequences for American-born or American-reared children. The loose structure and the fact that webs of contacts are not closed and all-encompassing tend to preclude the type of control and direction that would impact the lives of children. In many cases, the children of Filipino immigrants may have socioeconomic advantages that make social capital less important for them than for other groups, but the relatively loose networks with numerous bridges may also at least partially account for the fact that although Filipino American children display fairly high levels of school achievement by general American standards, those levels are actually lower than those of many other Asian American students.

Immigrant Family Network Forms in Context

In selecting immigrant groups as examples of different types of family networks, there is some danger of over-generalizing and stereotyping. Therefore, it should be kept in mind that there are wide variations within each group. Still, there are broad commonalities in family forms within groups and variations across groups. The differing family forms are not simply results of differing cultural heritages. Instead, they are consequences of contexts of exit and reception. More specifically, family structures are affected by how people leave their home countries and where they fit in to the society and economy of the host country.

Families do not exist only in the general setting of international relations and shifting labor markets, though. They also occupy places in specific localities, surrounded by neighbors and contacts. Families are important parts of social networks, but they are only parts. In order to describe other parts of immigrant networks and to consider how they can enable adaptation in varying ways, Chapter 5 will turn to where families live: to enclaves, neighborhoods, and communities.

5

Enclaves, Neighborhoods, and
Communities

This chapter looks at immigrant networks beyond and around families. The surrounding social relations will be considered here as consisting of three ideal types: enclaves, neighborhoods, and communities. Among these three, the enclave comes closest to the dense, bounded web of interconnections considered as a primary source of social capital. The idea of an ethnic enclave or an immigrant enclave is often specifically associated with that of the enclave economy. Alejandro Portes, arguably the most important theorist of the enclave economy, has defined it in terms of participation and location. According to Portes (1981: 290–1):

> Enclaves consist of immigrant groups which concentrate in a distinct spatial location and organize a variety of enterprises serving their own ethnic market and/or the general population. Their basic characteristic is that a significant portion of the immigrant labor force works in enterprises owned by other immigrants [of the same group].

Along these lines, Portes and Jensen (1992: 419) describe the immigrant enclave economy in terms of economic resources produced by social connections, when they define the enclave economy as "a concentrated network of ethnic firms" resulting in "jobs [for immigrant employees] and opportunities for entrepreneurship [among immigrant business owners]." The ties of potential immigrant entrepreneurs to co-ethnic workers, in this view, give the entrepreneurs a competitive business advantage.

The workers, on the other hand, enjoy access to jobs that would not otherwise be available to them. All participants in enclave businesses benefit from links to other businesses in the enclave and from a customer base among group members.

The benefits of enclave economies have been challenged on a number of grounds. One of the principal grounds has concerned the question of whose figurative account receives the social capital of immigrant relationships. This objection is frequently associated with the work of Sanders and Nee (1987), who argued that entrepreneurs in an enclave economy benefitted from cheap labor, but that enclave employees generally earned less than they would in the mainstream economy. This is essentially a special case of the debate over whether networks constrain or enable, but the argument here is that enclave economies enable entrepreneurs by constraining the opportunities of their workers through unequal structures of ties. Responding to this argument, Zhou and Logan (1989) argued that benefits to workers depend on the specific situation of the enclave economy of a particular immigrant group. One of the reasons that it is difficult to determine whether enclave entrepreneurs benefit at the expense of workers, which would be a case of the "dark side" of social capital, is that it is hard to know what the alternatives for individual workers might be. Workers in an enclave economy might well show lower earnings than similar workers in mainstream businesses, but the former could have little access to jobs in the mainstream, which could only absorb a limited number of immigrant employees.

Immigrant economic activities approach an economic enclave to the extent that they take place in a specific location occupied by an immigrant group and involve both labor and capital produced by group members in business institutions owned and controlled by members of the group. Immigrants engage in an enclave economy to the extent that they interact with the larger economy as self-contained units. Some immigrant economic activities may only approach an enclave in limited ways, as, for example, when immigrants use co-ethnic capital and labor for small businesses located outside of immigrant residential areas.

Viewed in this way, the immigrant economic enclave is one

dimension of an enclave defined as a relatively complete and self-contained immigrant society. This broader use of the idea of an enclave has some currency in contemporary writing on immigrants and their networks, although different authors have emphasized different aspects of the enclave as a distinctive, self-contained, geographically identifiable, internally interconnected social entity. Kim (2012), for example, described immigrants as constituting an enclave in the degree to which they are detached and secluded from the larger society, that is, to the extent that their networks have distinctive boundaries because ties exist chiefly among members of the immigrant group. Alba, Logan, and Crowder (1997) operationalized the enclave in terms of residential concentration, using the heavy overrepresentation of immigrants within a Census tract. Using concepts drawn from the economic enclave model, though, self-containment and concentration are only some of the definitional traits of an immigrant enclave. It should also be home to individuals who are highly interconnected and have their own institutions. A network analysis of an immigrant enclave should attempt to identify the pattern of interpersonal and institutional relations within a relatively detached residential concentration and to examine how that pattern influences linkages to the larger society on the part of the group as a whole and individuals within the group.

Since an enclave has a geographic basis, it is contained within the wider concept of the neighborhood. The precise meaning and nature of a "neighborhood" may be contested (Sampson, 2012), particularly given the modern detachment of interpersonal ties from place noted by Wellman (1999). For the purposes of the present book, though, we can define a neighborhood as a residential area; an immigrant neighborhood would be a residential area identified with immigrants. In theory, one can imagine a neighborhood that is not the basis of any interpersonal connections. In fact, there are many neighborhoods in which people have very few interactions with each other. Even in locations in which immigrants are in constant contact and communication, the neighborhood may not be considered an enclave, in the sense of a highly interconnected and self-contained society, because the immigrants also have extensive social contacts outside the neighborhood, because ties to neighbors are relatively weak, or because the neighborhood lacks participation in immigrant-based institutions. From a network perspective, though, a residential area is a relevant concept because it is a product of social connections and a basis for social connections. Asking whether people who live in a given neighborhood are linked to each other by strong and transitive ties is meaningful, as is investigating the extent to which their social connections are bounded by place of residence.

The concentration or dispersion of immigrant neighborhoods varies historically and across groups. Looking at immigrant groups settled in New York, Andrew Beveridge (2002) found that late twentieth-century (1990) neighborhood settlements were more spatially dispersed than early twentieth-century (1910) settlements. Those of the later period were much less likely to be concentrated in the central city. In my own work, I have described a suburban Vietnamese settlement that was residentially highly concentrated (Zhou and Bankston, 1998) and a Lao settlement (Bankston, 2006) in suburban pockets around a small town, with connections to an institutional center outside of town.

In addition to how concentrated an immigrant neighborhood is, the socioeconomic setting affects the structures of social relations and poses the challenges to which social networks respond. One of the primary tenets of the segmented assimilation argument is that immigrants since the 1970s have frequently settled in lower-income neighborhoods, troubled by joblessness and perceptions of lack of opportunity. Therefore, according to this argument, immigrant networks can provide alternatives to troubled socioeconomic surroundings. For adults, immigrant networks can offer mutual economic assistance and social-psychological supports. For children, immigrant networks can offer structured channels to upward mobility through education and can enable young people to bypass many of the social problems that plague those growing up in disadvantaged areas.

A community, in network terms, is a set of social ties (Wellman, 1999; Wierzbicki, 2004). The broader idea of a community, encompassing residential locations, is useful because place of residence is not the only basis for social interactions among immigrants or others. For example, members of an immigrant group may live scattered around a metropolitan area, but come together once a week in a religious institution, and that weekly meeting may be extremely important for their social ties and for their exchange of information or resources; or people may become members of an association or an informal club because of their immigrant origins, and thereby maintain relationships. With modern means of communication, it is even possible for immigrants to be widely spread across the nation and maintain contact and exchange support through telephones and the internet.

Whether immigrant networks are densely interconnected enclaves, shared places of residence, or network ties only loosely based on location, their consequences depend on the access of group members to information and opportunities and on the structures of relationships within the networks. No delimited set of connections among individuals, moreover, exists in isolation. This last point does not mean only that every immigrant community has some sort of bridging ties to people in the host society. It also means that immigrant communities nearly always have connections to other immigrant communities: particular settlements or sets of connections are generally linked to others. When one examines the organization of a neighborhood or a kinship or associational web, it is important to recognize, then, that it exists within linkages between communities that shape secondary migration, flows of information and resources, and perceptions of ethnic identity.

Neighborhoods and Networks in the Spanish-Speaking Working Class: Class and Communication

Contemporary Latino immigrant settlements in the United States exist because the immigrants seek jobs, and the jobs available to them are heavily concentrated in industries such as construction, meat-packing, textiles, and agricultural labor. The rise of the new destinations, moreover, has contributed to high geographic mobility, so that this mobility and high population turnover are common characteristics of Latino immigrant neighborhoods. In addition, the large numbers of undocumented immigrants from Mexico and Latin America limit links to the surrounding society and affect social cohesion within immigrant settlements.

Chapter 4 cited Wierzbicki's (2004) finding that immigrants had relatively small networks, especially kinship networks, as a result of their recent arrival. I have also suggested that the evidence indicates that movement away from the border areas and into the growing new destinations tends to take place along the lines of relatively weak ties, with small nuclear family groups following labor migrants. While most studies support the idea that relatively weak non-kin ties predominate in Latin American immigrant neighborhoods, there are some differences in findings on the sizes of Latin American social networks, possibly because of differences among neighborhoods in different parts of the country.

Looking at Mexican American neighborhoods in Chicago, Almeida et al. (2009) distinguished between social ties (the number of people to whom individuals were connected) and social cohesion. These researchers measured the latter based on perceptions of neighborhoods as close-knit, perceptions of the willingness of neighbors to help each other and of their getting along with each other, and perceptions of shared values and mutual trust. Almeida et al. found that living in a Mexican-concentration neighborhood was associated with large networks, in the sense of having many co-ethnic ties. However, the researchers found an inverse relationship between a neighborhood concentration of Mexicans and an individual's perception of social cohesion. If one thinks of an enclave as a place where people not only have many connections to each other, but have connections that communicate intense normative constraints and supports, then it becomes clear that residential concentrations alone do not constitute enclaves in this sense. To the extent that Mexican immigrant neighborhoods resemble those in this study, they do provide connections with co-ethnics, but those connections do not result in strong supports and constraints. Social networks, in such cases, do not automatically translate into social capital.

Not only do community networks not translate automatically into social capital, but social investments have different pay-offs, depending on what kind of resources and information communities can produce. Studying social networking in a new destination in northeastern Oklahoma, Carlos Garcia (2005) found that his respondents had three subnetworks. One of these was a traditional subnetwork of relatives and friends living in the community known as El Tree. All of Garcia's residents agreed that it was much more difficult to find work or housing without the help of friends or relatives. Garcia also found that immigrants relied on a church subnetwork and a contract subnetwork of labor recruiters. All of these networks, though, were essentially yielding the same asset: a working-class job, mainly in the local meat-packing plant. As discussed in Chapter 3, new working-class jobs of this sort are the main contemporary reason for drawing Latino immigrants to the United States. Therefore, even apart from the density of ties and intensity of solidarity in Latino neighborhoods, the information available for transmission along the lines of those ties is information about jobs in this new working class. In Garcia's study, mutual assistance and obligations reinforced occupational specialization. He quotes respondents who reported they felt they could honor the co-ethnics who had helped them find work by carrying out their jobs conscientiously, and that they could pass on the assistance by bringing others into the same workplaces. Community networks promoted not upward mobility but occupational entrenchment, because of the industrial orientation of neighborhoods created by patterns of migration and settlement within the structure of ethnic stratification.

The tendency of Latin American immigrant residential concentrations to form around specific industries means that the social networks in these concentrations channel network participants toward work in the same industries. While the location-based networks enable people to find work as construction laborers, meat packers, or carpet makers, these interpersonal connections also constrain them from finding other kinds of work. There is, however, another important consequence of concentration in the same types of work. Rubén Hernández-León (2007: 1152) pointed out in a review symposium of Ivan Light's (2006) important book on shifting places of immigration:

> In contrast to existing scholarship on migration networks which insists that an immigrant's greatest ally is another immigrant, *Deflecting Immigration* suggests the opposite, namely, that an immigrant's greatest rival is (or potentially can be) a co-ethnic immigrant, especially if both are poor. They are rivals in that they will compete for the same jobs, creating an oversupply of labour that will eventually lower wages, and for the same housing, driving up the cost of rentals and exhausting the supply of residences.

Being competitors for jobs and housing tends to lower collaboration and the social solidarity that lies behind collaboration. In the earlier stages of arrival in a new destination, interpersonal competition among the residents of an emerging immigrant residential concentration may be relatively low. In this early stage, the evidence indicates that new arrivals will be finding work and homes disproportionately through relatively weak ties, so that the social connections may be fairly effective in communicating information about a limited set of opportunities, but will not provide high levels of cooperation in creating opportunities and will produce fairly low levels of solidarity. As more immigrants seek jobs in the same workplaces, neighbors will help each other out of friendship and a sense of common ethnic origin, but competition will act as a brake on their development of inter-reliant patterns of support.

While contemporary Latin American immigrants are undoubtedly unique in many ways, they also illustrate more general network forces at work in immigrant residential areas. Other things being equal, geographic mobility, in the form of large numbers of continual new arrivals and in the form of secondary migration, tends to lead to relatively weak ties in immigrant settlements. Bridging ties to the larger society primarily occur through individuals who have found working-class jobs. Occupational concentration of an immigrant group limits the information that can be conveyed through networks, particularly when the concentration is in the lower socioeconomic strata. Immigrants who are in the same types of jobs all share the same kinds of information, so that their communities do not constitute differentiated networks. Those who do the same work are also potential competitors, so that social ties may not produce high levels of solidarity or cooperation.

Korean Communities: Solidarity and the Creation of Social Capital

Although concentrated Korean residential enclaves are not common in the United States, residential communities that come close to being enclaves do exist, most notably in southern California. In her work on how neighborhoods matter for the education of immigrant children, Min Zhou (2009) has provided a description of the Koreatown in Los Angeles. In Zhou's account, although this Koreatown actually has a large Hispanic population, its Korean population maintains high solidarity and communicates social capital to its children through interlocking non-profit community-based organizations, churches and other religious institutions, ethnic professional organizations, local businesses, Korean-language media, and youth community centers.

Linda Trinh Vo and Mary Yu Danico (2004) give a similar, more comprehensive account of another Koreatown in nearby Orange County, an outgrowth of the Los Angeles settlement that began in the 1970s, as Koreans who had arrived first in Los Angeles moved out. From 1980 to 1990, the Korean population of Orange County grew from 11,339 to 35,919. Korean merchants in Los Angeles were especial targets of the 1992 Los Angeles riots, and this encouraged additional movement by Koreans seeking a safer place to establish their families, homes, and businesses (Vo and Danico, 2004).

In the previous section, I argued that lack of economic differentiation, resulting from labor market placement, tends to limit the type of information and the levels of solidarity-based cooperation within community networks. While the heavy concentration of Koreans in small-business self-employment, in Orange County's Koreatown and elsewhere, could give rise to some competition among co-ethnics, these entrepreneurs engage in a wide range of business activities. The area is thus a highly differentiated shopping district. Moreover, it is also a residential location. Vo and Danico (2004: 23) describe Koreatown and nearby Little Saigon as "self-sufficient communities providing ethnics with all their entertainment, shopping, media, professional services, and other needs."

Koreatown is, interestingly, not entirely or even mostly made up of Koreans. According to one journalistic source (Kim, 2003), in the early twenty-first century, Koreans constituted only 20 percent of the residents in Koreatown: most of the others were Latino. The ways that Latinos (and Latino networks) linked to Korean networks will be explored in the section on social capital and ethnic specialization in Chapter 7, but for now it should be noted that an ethnic enclave economy rests on a geographic clustering of members of an ethnic group and an arrangement of economic ties among members of that group, but the enclave does not require the absence of others. It only requires that the most significant economic ties be among ethnic group members.

Koreatown's enclave economy is best seen as a core part of its residential enclave: the movement of Korean immigrants into a residential concentration formed the basis of the business activities. Because Koreans live there, they provided a dedicated source of customers for ethnic enterprises. As Koreatown expanded, it attracted more immigrants arriving directly from Korea, and these new arrivals, along with the family workers discussed in Chapter 4, supplied comparatively inexpensive labor. While family loans were an important source of capital, rotating credit associations, involving the pooling of funds among co-ethnics, were another major source. Beyond the local network, though, transnational connections offered a more distant source of capital, from South Korean investors who saw co-ethnics as dependable investment opportunities in the United States (Vo and Danico, 2004). Thus, a differentiated residential clustering combined with connections across countries to translate community ties into financial assets.

One of the interesting developments in the Korean settlement in Orange County has been the emergence of satellite Korean clusters.

Indeed, the Orange County Koreatown itself initially came into existence at least in part as a satellite of nearby Los Angeles. Koreans have tended to settle in areas around Koreatown, establishing small ethnic clusters in suburbs such as Anaheim, Buena Park, Fullerton, and Irvine (Vo and Danico, 2004). It is possible that these ethnic satellite settlements will become more important centers than Koreatown for those in them, but the Orange County neighborhood remains a vital center for the others. These satellite clusters, along with the fact that Koreans do not actually make up most of the population of Koreatown, suggest some of the ways in which the Orange County concentration, in spite of some unique characteristics, represents some broader characteristics of Korean community networks in the United States and of many apparently dispersed suburban immigrant networks in general.

While the Orange County Koreatown presents a variant on the ethnic enclave among Koreans, most first-generation Koreans have differed from this example in two respects. First, the most common pattern for Korean entrepreneurs has not been stores that serve co-ethnics, but enterprises that serve (and often employ) members of other ethnic and racial groups. Second, Korean immigrants to the United States most often do not live in ethnic neighborhoods around their businesses, as one would expect in an ethnic enclave, but in neighborhoods away from their businesses, frequently among members of other ethnic groups.

Even in Koreatown, Korean merchants hire non-Korean (mostly Latino) employees and they serve large numbers of non-Korean shoppers. In most other parts of the United States, though, the most common Korean entrepreneurial activities have consisted of shop-owners serving members of other groups, mostly minority groups. Indeed, this has been the pattern in Los Angeles, and African American resentment of Korean businesses in black neighborhoods fueled the attacks on Korean shops in 1992 that pushed many Koreans to relocate to Orange County. This very fact, though, indicates that much of the capital that flowed into Orange County to develop Koreatown came from profits in non-Korean neighborhoods in Los Angeles.

At the level of networks linking communities, the connections between Los Angeles and Orange County are reminders that the functioning of immigrant networks in geographical space depends on how those are connected to each other and on the flows of resources and information among them. These connections across locations illustrate the fact that immigrant networks consist of ties among people that are structured by linkages among communities. In particular, the satellite ethnoburbs demonstrate that apparent dispersions are often actually geographically wide sets of network connections.

In a conference paper presented in 2007, Sookhee Oh offered intriguing findings on the suburban settlement of Korean immigrants in the New York metropolitan area. Looking at the fast-growing settlement of Korean immigrants in New Jersey's suburban Bergen County, Oh held that the ethnic ties of these Korean immigrants had been maintained not only by the fact that their significant social connections were most often to other Koreans living nearby in the suburbs, but also by the fact that all had consumption linkages for ethnic goods at Korean shops in New York City and elsewhere.

Regardless of whether Korean communities are tethered by an identifiable enclave-type center, such as Koreatown, the community networks that can be identified with them have tended to be these sort of satellite variants on the ethnic enclave. Their businesses serve non-Korean more often than Korean customers, but capital and support to these businesses radiate inward from ethnic sources: family members, loans from Korean American organizations, and investors in Korea. Similarly, the connections to each other derive from geographical centers that radiate outward: shops that sell Korean goods or institutions and places that serve as focal points for Korean identification and social organization.

Ethnic Enclaves and Solidarity: The Vietnamese American Example

Among the four groups used as primary illustrations of immigrant social networks, Vietnamese Americans come closest to the enclave, as derived from the enclave economy theory developed by Alejandro Portes. Portes attributed the economic success of the south Florida Cuban immigrant community to the social ties within geographically concentrated locations that gave Cuban entrepreneurs privileged access to Cuban workers and, initially, to Cuban customers. By reinvesting the financial capital created by this social capital, the Cubans created a flourishing economy in south Florida, which could then sell products and services to customers outside the enclave and generate even more financial capital. In the process, the enclave economy created more jobs for Cubans within it, although, as noted in Chapter 2 in the discussion of problems with immigrant networks as sources of social capital, the extent to which workers, as cheap labor in an ethnic economy, benefitted is a matter of substantial debate.

Min Zhou's (1992) description of New York's Chinatown as an urban enclave developed and extended Portes's ideas. Zhou argued that Chinese employers in Chinatown, like the Cuban entrepreneurs in Florida, provided jobs for newly arrived immigrants, whose labor enabled the employers to build and maintain profitable businesses. Zhou placed even more emphasis than Portes did on ethnic community networks, arguing that ties to family members and others in the Chinese community enabled immigrants not simply to survive in low-paid jobs, but to advance in American society. The normative expectations embedded in those social ties encouraged work and saving, and this contributed to the success of ethnic enterprises and to gradual upward mobility on the part of individuals.

Min Zhou and I (1998) extended the enclave social network further to describe Vietnamese American communities. Combining a national-level account of the emergence of Vietnamese communities in the United States with a case study of a highly concentrated Vietnamese residential enclave in New Orleans, we argued that social networks in Vietnamese residential communities had been critical for the adaptation of the members of this new immigrant group. Although there is an ethnic business district in the neighborhood we used as our case study, entrepreneurship was less central to our description of this enclave than it was to either the original formulation by Portes or the application of enclave concepts to Chinatown in Zhou's earlier work. In addition, we were chiefly interested in how network connections provided direction, constraint, and support to young people, so our focus shifted from the enclave as an economic unit to the enclave as a source of social investment in children.

In looking at Latin American community ties, I emphasized the influence of the context of immigration, specifically geographic proximity and the rise of the new Spanish-speaking working class, in shaping patterns of immigrant social relations. The context of immigration for the Vietnamese has been quite different. The initial U.S. government effort to scatter Vietnamese refugees around the United States, followed by condensation into Vietnamese settlements across the country as newcomers suddenly arriving from a vastly different society sought familiarity and mutual support, created concentrated ethnic pockets spread around the different states.

A 1993 Office of Refugee Resettlement study (United States Department of Health and Human Services, 1993) found that Vietnamese community formation consisted of three phases. First, an initial wave of war exiles, mostly from middle-class backgrounds, arrived from 1975 to 1979. In spite of the government effort to scatter them around, these individuals began regrouping and establishing identifiable immigrant settlements. Second, from 1979 to 1982, many more refugees arrived. The larger influx included the rural poor and the Sino-Vietnamese, a disproportionate number of whom had been shop-keepers and entrepreneurs in Vietnam. Third, during the 1980s, self-organizing Vietnamese communities developed, absorbing new arrivals.

The single largest Vietnamese pocket is Orange County's Little Saigon, although there are a number of other settlements, notably in Houston, that are also known as "Little Saigon" because they are Vietnamese American business and residential centers (Vo and Danico, 2004). These centers came into existence as part of the emergence of a national pattern of Vietnamese American communities. Min Zhou and I (1998) noted that massive secondary migration, by refugees seeking mutual material and psychological support, first brought these communities into existence, and that new international arrivals then tended to gravitate toward those locations where they had contacts. As a result,

[b]y 1990, almost half the Vietnamese had settled in California alone, and about a third lived in the other nine states on the top ten list ... Within states, the Vietnamese have also clustered in just a few metropolitan areas ... Moreover, this same tendency to cluster occurred within metropolitan areas, so that the Vietnamese often found themselves living in neighborhoods that had large proportions of co-ethnics. (Zhou and Bankston, 1998: 47–8)

Describing the cross-community connections, one of my informants once remarked that many Vietnamese Americans tend to see the United States as a vast arrangement of Vietnamese neighborhoods connected by highways. While this type of network across communities is necessarily looser than the web of ties of individuals in a residential enclave, the extent to which communities maintain links with each other has empirical social capital implications. For example, when New Orleans was devastated by Hurricane Katrina in 2005, the New Orleans Vietnamese were able to temporarily relocate to other Vietnamese communities (chiefly the one in Houston) because of their existing ethnic support groups in those other locations, and they were able to return and rebuild their homes more quickly than many other New Orleanians because of that cross-community-level network support (Airriess et al., 2008; Vu et al., 2009). Similarly, Park et al. (2010: 88) report that for the Vietnamese in Biloxi, Mississippi, after Hurricane Katrina, "[a]long with NGOs, the local institutions, and family and friends across the country, the national networks of Vietnamese American organizations became important sources of support and aid."

There can be a darker side to networks of immigrant communities. On the matter of "negative social capital," these inter-community linkages have also facilitated the flow of less desirable forms of information and resources: "One of the [youth] gangs that was identified to us ... was believed to have connections with Vietnamese criminal organizations in Biloxi, Mississippi. The close ties among the Vietnamese communities scattered around the country provided a natural network for the delinquents in their communities" (Zhou and Bankston, 1998: 190).

The networks of Vietnamese communities across the United States largely came into existence because the Southeast Asian refugee resettlement program brought so many people to the country in such a short period of time (mainly in the 1980s), because of the initial unfamiliarity of the Vietnamese in the U.S., and because of the secondary migration that contributed to the creation of nationwide networks. These same contextual determinants were also important in forming the individual immigrant enclaves within the broader geographic web. Within the settlements, culture did contribute to the development of differentiated, interconnected networks. One can identify ideas about kinship relations (discussed in Chapter 4) and religious organizations (discussed in Chapter 6) as some of the major cultural elements. However, immigrants tend to draw on cultural traditions and remake them in response to the environment of the new homeland, as I've pointed out in Chapter 4, on family ties. Beyond culture, the pattern of refugee resettlement, within the arrival of large numbers of people and their clustering together, helped to develop differentiated and institutionally complete community networks. Notably, an initial arrival primarily by members of the middle class, who established settlements for receiving and organizing the larger numbers of refugees, helped to form differentiated and interdependent immigrant societies.

This pattern of refugee resettlement was similar to that of another refugee group of quite different cultural background: the Cubans. Both the Cubans and the Vietnamese, as refugees, arrived with particular kinds of bridging ties, since they received settlement assistance from the U.S. government. In addition to giving material support that helped refugee groups establish communities, the refugee process contributed to the internal structuring of their community networks, though. As described by Alejandro Portes (1981), the clustering and rapid growth of the Cuban American population also consisted of early institutional establishment by members of the middle class, and the Cuban refugee population grew within this institutional establishment, creating internally differentiated social networks. This similarity to the Vietnamese was the main reason that Min Zhou and I drew so heavily on the social capital concepts developed by Portes in his work on the Cubans. It should serve as a reminder that the adaptation of different groups of immigrants can be seen as historical variations on a set of network principles, rather than as unique outcomes for culturally differing immigrant nationalities.

The area around Orange County's Little Saigon, the Vietnamese American enclave with the greatest similarities to Miami's Little Havana, was home to an estimated 88,000 Vietnamese residents in 2010 (Bankston, forthcoming(b)). The Little Saigon business district boasts shops and restaurants of nearly every category. It also has a Vietnamese Chamber of Commerce, social service organizations, Buddhist temples, Vietnamese Catholic churches, and a network of Vietnamese language schools for children, and holds regular celebrations of Vietnamese holidays. It has its own Vietnamese-language newspapers, and is the headquarters for Vietnam California Radio and Saigon TV, the most popular Vietnamese-language television channel in the U.S., with local affiliates in Los Angeles, San Francisco, and San Jose, as well as nationwide satellite availability (Bankston, forthcoming(b)). It is, in other words, almost a complete society in itself.

In our case study of a smaller Vietnamese community, Min Zhou and I described how an immigrant enclave community can function as a network to generate assets for those in it. The reconstructed (and sometimes constructed) kinship networks that I described in Chapter 4 exist within a broader web of relationships among neighbors and participation in local ethnic economic activities, including loans and shared labor among co-ethnics, as well as shopping in Vietnamese businesses. As we point out, economic relations of the face-to-face sort are also fundamentally social relations and bind people together. Further, "the economic activities in the Vietnamese community not only enable families to be self-sufficient but also help finance community-based organizations and keep capital within the ethnic network of social relations" (Zhou and Bankston, 1998: 104). People who live together and work together closely may not always like each other, but they do give each other trust (and credit, which is the financial version of trust). These ties focus on organizations, most notably the church in this particular Catholic community, but also civic organizations such as the Vietnamese Voters' Association.

The benefits of this type of interlocking community network will be discussed in more detail in Chapter 6, in looking at formal organizations, and in Chapters 7 and 8, on economic and academic adaptation; but, first, it will be helpful to make qualifications of what could otherwise be an overly enthusiastic endorsement of tightly knit immigrant enclaves in general and of Vietnamese residential enclaves in particular. The first qualification concerns another aspect of the "dark side of social capital," and another involves a hedging of the view that all Vietnamese communities or all immigrant communities with backgrounds similar to those of the Vietnamese will be completely formed enclaves.

The dense, transitive webs of interlocking social ties that provide support and collective direction can also be sources of tension and exclusion. Vietnamese Americans often do not like to discuss factions among community members with outsiders, but bitter dissensions can arise in settings in which everyone knows everyone else and expects agreement from everyone else. Some of my respondents have on a number of occasions remarked on factions forming around competing leaders. In the area around southern California's Little Saigon, Tony Lam, a member of the Westminster City Council and the first Vietnamese American elected official, became a target of his community's intense demand for conformity in 1999 when he refused to take part in a demonstration against a video store that had displayed a picture of Ho Chi Minh. Among young people, this demand for conformity can manifest itself through the imposition by family, neighbors, and institutions of strict rules regarding matters such as gender roles (Bankston, 1995). The network linkages that lock some in can, by the same token, lock non-conformists out, so that juvenile delinquency is often as much a matter of rejection of non-conforming youth by adult networks as it is a matter of information and influences moving among Vietnamese communities (Bankston and Caldas, 1996; Bankston and Zhou, 1997).

Vietnamese American communities realize the concept of an immigrant enclave to different extents. This, also, is a point that yields an important generalization about immigrant networks and social capital. Forms of community relations depend on particular settings and circumstances, as well as on international and national contexts of migration. Park et al. (2010), studying the recovery of the Vietnamese of Biloxi following Hurricane Katrina, found that although their respondents had a strong sense of community and mutual obligation, they were having trouble rebuilding their neighborhood. Doctoral candidate Vy Dao has been engaged in a comparative study of three Gulf Coast Vietnamese communities and has found that the Biloxi Vietnamese have less mutual coordination among neighbors than the New Orleans Vietnamese, in part because the residences of the former constitute less of a centralized, concentrated geographic enclave than those of the latter. Those in Biloxi are more spread out in small clusters (Dao, n.d.). These differing degrees of community concentration are apparently consequences of local circumstances. The Vietnamese enclave in New Orleans formed on the basis of available empty housing on the edge of the city (Zhou and Bankston, 1998). The Vietnamese in Biloxi initially tried to settle in close proximity, but the development of the casino industry encouraged Gulf Coast real estate development and drove up housing prices in the Vietnamese residential areas, resulting in greater dispersion, with apparent consequences for the utilization of social networks (Bankston, 2012b).

The example of Vietnamese American immigrants illustrates the paradoxical network consequences that can often follow mass refugee-type migration of groups as culturally varied as the Vietnamese and the Cubans. The clustering of refugees seeking mutual assistance for adaptation to a new country in which they do not have a pre-existing socioeconomic position in the host country structure can throw them back on their own social resources, leading to the creation of interdependent immigrant enclave-style communities and strong ethnic networks. In addition, the example illustrates the phenomenon of community-level networks, which can be understood as networks of networks.

"Assimilated" Immigrant Communities

A number of immigrant groups are outwardly assimilated in many respects, and yet retain not only strong ethnic identification but links to other group members. Outwardly assimilated groups may include those with large numbers of professionally employed individuals, such as segments of the South Asian immigrant population, and marital migrants, who enter as spouses of citizens and residents. Immigrants from the Philippines can illustrate community networks among the outwardly assimilated of these two major categories (see the discussion of Filipino professional migrants and marital migrants in Chapter 4).

Outwardly assimilated groups often do have some spatially identifiable ethnic residential areas, and these can serve as symbolic centers for those living elsewhere. For Filipinos in the United States, the most significant geographic symbolic center is Historic Filipinotown in Los Angeles, which was a central location for the arrival of Filipinos in the United States in the 1950s and 1960s (Macatuno, 2002). About 7,000 people identified as Filipinos still lived in Historic Filipinotown by the time of the 2000 U.S. Census, although the majority population was Latino by that time (Bankston, 2006). Other historic Filipino enclaves include the old Filipino neighborhood of San Francisco (now represented by Manilatown Center) and the remnants of Little Manila in Stockton (Macatuno, 2002; Broom, 2003; Bankston, 2006).

Although the Filipinotowns, Manilatowns, and Little Manilas of an earlier era are now largely memories of a time when Filipino immigrants settled in enclaves similar in some respects to today's Little Saigons, there is still a geographic element to Filipino immigrant settlement, as there is for many other outwardly assimilated groups. California contains by far the largest number of Filipinos, about half of those living in the United States. Moreover, Los Angeles County is the most significant concentration, as it is for a variety of immigrant groups, since it was home to over 262,000 residents identified as Filipinos in 2000 (Bankston, 2006). Nearly all the Filipinos spread across the United States, including the professional migrants and the marital migrants, have friends and family living in the Los Angeles area, a fact that underscores the importance of inter-community networks.

Despite the preponderance of Filipino immigrants in California, especially in southern California, most Filipinos in the United States do not live in identifiable Filipino neighborhoods. The one-third of married Filipino immigrant women who had American-born spouses (see Chapter 4) had little motivation to live in separate ethnic enclaves. The medical personnel, accountants, engineers, and teachers (see Chapter 3) had little need to band together with co-ethnics for mutual support, and they needed to live near their jobs in locations around the country.

In an article published over two decades ago, Liu et al. (1991) maintained that the two main sources of immigration from the Philippines, namely family-based migration and occupational migration, constituted two distinct migration chains and that the former was likely to lead to the rejuvenation of older Filipino American communities. However, as I have pointed out in Chapter 4, marriage migration, often through marriage to native-born Americans, played an important part in family-based migration, increasing the connections to the larger American society of even those who enter by means of family connections. The high level of exogamy by immigrant women from the Philippines, in particular, means that there are very few Filipino Americans who do not include some out-married Filipino women in their family and friendship circles. This includes even those who do live in the locations that contain large numbers of Filipinos. Thus, all Filipino community networks have indistinct boundaries. Moreover, the two sources of migration overlap heavily due to personal inter-connections among Filipino immigrants, regardless of mode of immigration.

If Vietnamese immigrant communities can be taken as illustrating variations on networks as enclaves, Filipino communities may be understood as illustrating the phenomenon of indistinct network boundaries among groups with extensive personal and socioeconomic links to the larger society. One should not confuse indistinct boundaries with non-existence or unimportance, though. Throughout the United States, Filipino immigrants maintain ties to each other and keep track of new Filipinos arriving in their localities.

These interpersonal contacts have consequences. In a 2008 dissertation on the influence of role models on Filipino American identities, N. Judy Patacsil found that Filipino American college students maintained a sense of ethnic identity in large part as a consequence of their personal connections with other Filipinos. Connections with parents and other family members were the most important, but Filipino professionals in the United Students whom the students knew personally also shaped this sense of identity. As I will discuss in greater detail in Chapter 8, the interpersonal contacts, even though they lack the density and intensity of enclave linkages, can promote the accumulation of human capital.

Filipinos in the United States, living largely outside of ethnic enclaves and in close contact with people who are not Filipino, maintain their social connections in two ways. One of these is the informal network. The wives' circles that I mentioned in Chapter 4, on family networks, and Chapter 5, on community networks, constitute one prominent form of the informal network. The other, to be discussed in greater detail in Chapter 6, is the formal organization based on ethnicity. For now, it should be noted that people usually learn about formal organizations through their informal contacts, and that the formal organizations, in turn, sustain and strengthen interpersonal relations.

Basic Elements of Immigrant Community Networks

Looking at the primary examples, then, has yielded some general insights into the basic elements of community networks, and into how these can vary. One of these elements is location. Sets of connections among immigrants bring people to locations, and being together in the same place (a neighborhood) can maintain connections. The form of a set of social ties in a location, though, can be shaped by geographic mobility and by internal differentiation, with implications for the consequences of social relations.

Continual geographic mobility may, according to some evidence, limit the number of social ties and it often limits the strength of those ties. Since mutual interchange depends on meeting needs, the utility of a network depends on the assets that those participating in it can offer each other. If they are all employees, seeking the same jobs in the host society, they may be able to offer little more than information about where to find positions within a socioeconomic level. Moreover, immigrants in the position of seeking the same opportunities from the host society will normally compete with each other, so that their interconnections will produce relatively few assets.

Immigrant communities never exist in isolation. This is not just because of secondary migration or the ties of individuals in some locations or webs of associations to other individuals. It is also because immigrant communities tend to be networks of networks, and how one community functions depends on how it is linked to others. The traditional view of immigrant settlement is of people living in heavily settled urban centers, but highly interconnected networks in the more suburban arrangements of modern metropolitan areas can involve clusters linked together by shopping districts or symbolic centers. Social proximity, further, is not the same as geographic proximity. The "middleman minority" problem can be understood as one of occupational specialization creating a gap between the two: the meaningful links of middleman minority shop-owners are mostly to members of their own group, even though the shops exist physically in the midst of neighborhoods to which the owners have few immediate social connections.

The immigrant communities that most closely approximate the ethnic enclave are frequently experiencing the shock of the new, with few existing ties to the host society and no predefined places in it. Immigrants who arrive as refugees, then, often tend to be among those who form enclaves, although others may also experience newness and the need to create their own social locations. The extent to which a specific community approaches an enclave will be affected by local circumstances, as well as by the general context of entry. Because the mutual interdependence of enclaves can be adaptive, disadvantage can be turned into a kind of advantage. For a fully interdependent enclave community, though, some measure of internal network differentiation is required. Again, immigrant communities exist as networks across community networks, and the same lack of familiarity with the host society that can create enclaves also frequently creates connections among enclaves.

Finally, even members of the most outwardly assimilated immigrant groups often maintain social networks that affect adaptation. Those with extensive personal and occupational connections to the host society maintain ethnic networks that have indistinct boundaries, but still exist and affect their lives. These networks are maintained by informal interpersonal circles, but also by formal organizations.

6

The Role of Formal Institutions

In one of his early works on the nature of social networks, Scott Feld (1981) sought to account for the origins of social circles by pointing out that individuals organize their social relations around what he called "foci." "A focus," he explained, "is defined as a social, psychological, or legal entity around which joint activities are organized (e.g., workplaces, voluntary organizations, hangouts, families, etc.). As a consequence of interaction associated with their joint activities, individuals whose activities are organized around the same focus will tend to become interpersonally tied and will form a cluster" (p. 1016).

Feld argues further that variations among foci produce variations in ties among network participants: "the structure of a network is dependent upon the constraint and size of the underlying foci. Highly constraining foci will create close-knit clusters of various sizes depending on the size of the foci" (1981: 1019). In addition, the numbers of foci in which individuals participate determine network characteristics. If two people are connected to each other through a focus, both are likely to be connected to any other person who is also connected to one of them through that focus, so that foci promote transitivity. Bridging ties, those that connect a network group member to someone outside the network, tend to be ties across different foci. The density of personal networks derives from the extent to which one's network is centered on a given focus.

One might see the influences on networks discussed in previous chapters in terms of foci. Families and communities, for example, are foci around which personal ties are formed. A set of friends with whom one meets on a regular basis is a focus. The indeterminate boundaries of some outwardly assimilated immigrant group members can be seen as the result of the members organizing their social lives around multiple foci: an occupational setting that includes mostly people not in the immigrant group, non-immigrant family members, or other friendship circles.

I bring the concept of the focus in at this point because there is one form of social organization to which the idea of a center of network orientation is particularly relevant. Formal institutions both give stable expression to network connections and serve as means of maintaining repeated interactions and of channeling social support, resources, and information. Clubs, voluntary and civic organizations, business associations, and religious institutions bring networks into sharp and well-defined focus among individuals and families and within different type of communities.

Weak Institutions: Sources and Consequences

An examination of formal institutions or organizations as network foci and producers of social capital should begin by distinguishing between organizations that arise from sets of interpersonal relations and organizations created outside these sets for purposes such as mobilizing or directing people or providing services to them. Examples of the former among immigrants would be a mutual assistance group that immigrants form in order to help each other, a rotating loan association, an ethnically based club, or a religious group formed by immigrants. Examples of the latter would be labor unions that seek to enroll immigrant workers, non-profit voluntary agencies that provide immigrant services, or churches proselytizing among immigrants or seeking immigrant members.

Although these kinds of organizations can be distinguished, they are not mutually exclusive. Consistent with the idea of a network focus, any externally created organization may create social circles by bringing immigrants together. Immigrants who join a labor union become part of a pre-existing institutional structure, but within this structure they may form their own ties to each other, and these ties, in turn, can serve as a basis for cooperation (social capital) within the workplace. Similarly, immigrants may be participants in an established religious organization, but form links with each other through their participation. Social networks, in other words, can grow within the shell of organizations created outside those networks. Indeed, this is part of what happens in the phenomenon that R. Stephen Warner (1994) has called "de facto congregationalism," the tendency of even hierarchical churches in the United States to become voluntary associations run by members.

Formal institutions among immigrants may also develop in the opposite direction: a mutual assistance group among immigrants, for instance, may become a service-providing organization offering help in finding employment, housing, or other benefits for immigrant group members who are primarily recipients of benefits, rather than active participants. Developments in both directions occur to varying degrees, though. A non-profit organization or a church or temple may serve immigrants without producing highly cooperative networks among them. Similarly, sets of interpersonal connections among immigrants may not necessarily result in a formal institutional arrangement, with the capacity for maintaining structured repeated interactions and for channeling support, resources, and information.

From the perspective of networks as sources of assets, the primary questions about formal institutions are: when do these produce collaborative social networks and under what conditions do networks result in effective organizational structures? When formally organized institutions encourage high levels of network collaboration and when networks can utilize these institutions to achieve desirable individual and collective outcomes, one can speak of strong institutions; that is, formal institutions that are closely bound to underlying social networks and that facilitate action by and through these networks.

One way to begin thinking about conditions that produce

strong institutions is to discuss why many immigrants may have relatively weak formal institutions. In discussing different types of communities in Chapter 5, I suggested that immigrants who arrive as refugees often form enclave-type settlements, with strong and dense ties among group members. One of the ways that such an enclave can establish and maintain high levels of cooperation and control is through its formal institutions. However, refugee groups do not of necessity lead to strong institutions.

Comparing Vietnamese, Lao, and Cambodian religious institutions through three case studies, Min Zhou, Rebecca Y. Kim, and I (Zhou et al., 2001) found that although all three showed some similarities in social functions, the Cambodian temple was by far the "weakest" of them, in the sense I am using that term here. Although the Vietnamese church and the Laotian and Cambodian temples we described were all ethnic network foci, only the last did not play a major role in the economic adaptation of its adherents. Based on our research, we accounted for the difference as follows: the Cambodians have suffered the most traumatic and drastic experiences in the troubled history of Southeast Asia. Haunted by memories of the genocidal Khmer Rouge years, they are chiefly concerned with mending their

> "broken hearts." . . . Their collective action still revolves around basic psychological adjustment, around trying to make some sense out of an anomic present and a chaotic past. A second characteristic that sets the Cambodian organization apart from the other two is the relative lack of lay control over the religious institution . . . Organizing committees and raising funds [in the Vietnamese and Laotian cases] tended to place power in the hands of laypeople charged with these responsibilities . . . The Cambodians, traumatized and confused, with low levels of income education, and home ownership, have relied on traditional authorities [i.e., the monks as institutional professionals]. (Zhou et al., 2001: 65)

It should be noted that many of the difficulties of the Cambodian refugees may have been overcome in the years since we completed this study (see Bankston, forthcoming(a), on current upward mobility among Cambodian Americans). However, in our comparative study, we found not only that Cambodian refugees in the United States still had relatively little in the way of information and resources to communicate with each other because of their continuing socioeconomic marginality, but that their extraordinarily traumatic context of migration contributed to prolonging this marginality by making it difficult for them to engage in ongoing productive interactions. The network structure, moreover, affected the kinds of formal institutions they established and how they related to these institutions. In a sense, of course, Cambodian Buddhist temples are all internal to the group: the monks and temple personnel are Cambodians and the funds to establish temples come from Cambodians. But the critical institutional activities fall chiefly to the monkhood as a professional establishment and lay management is (or was at the time of this study) fairly limited. There is (or was) not much "de facto congregationalism," with the institution directed by voluntary associations of members, with interpersonal networks operating through formal institutions. Thus, the Cambodian temple tended to be a "weak" institution, not closely bound to underlying networks that operated in and through it.

Cambodian immigrants have made up only a small part of the American immigrant population and their history is in many ways unique. Nevertheless, I think that one can use the ideas about institutions and networks developed here to consider the immigrant group that is by far the largest, and one that has served among the four groups used as bases for illustration in this book. Mexicans and immigrants from Mexico's southern neighbors have a history and migration context much different from the Cambodians', but the general view that context of migration shapes social networks and that fragmented social networks tend to lead to weak formal institutions is still relevant for many Latin American immigrants.

Latino communities within the United States do have community-based organizations. A large number of community development corporations (CDCs) have been involved in efforts to revitalize low-income Latino neighborhoods. However, even apart from the fact that most of those involved in CDCs have been native-born North Americans of Latin American ancestry, these

CDCs have primarily involved attempting to bring in investment from external sources such as banks, government, and foundations. While these organizations have been the efforts of local activists, they have not relied heavily on turning ethnic networks into financial capital (Brooke, 1999).

Among Latin American immigrants, as among the other groups discussed here, faith-based organizations often occupy central positions in communities. In a paper presented at the 2007 meeting of the American Sociological Association, Dinorah Manago reported that her research on Latino day laborers in New York City found that faith-based community organizations provided the greatest source of cultural stability and that these organizations shaped many of the shared experiences of these immigrants. Similarly, in a different geographic setting, Patricia Campion (2003) found that a Southern Baptist mission in southwestern Louisiana became a core community organization for Mexican immigrant workers.

While Protestant missions such as those Campion studied are making rapid inroads among Latin American immigrants, most of those immigrants continue to be Catholics, so that Catholic churches have become social support centers for new immigrant communities from Mexico and Central America. Along these lines, Mary E. Odem (2004), looking at a Catholic mission in Atlanta, found that the Catholic church provided immigrants with family and youth programs, English language classes, and job training, as well as religious ceremonies. Odem characterized these church endeavors as vital to ethnic community building. In my own preliminary examinations of the rapidly growing Latin American immigrant population of the New Orleans area, I have found the local Catholic Hispanic Apostolate to play an essential role as a provider of services and information (Bankston, 2009a; 2009b). In a dissertation on Latino immigration into Los Angeles, Cid Gregory Martinez (2009) argued that Latino immigrants, many of whom are undocumented, are marginalized in American society and that the Catholic church has become the location for providing services and enabling social exchange among immigrants.

Because of the undocumented status of many Latin American immigrants, because their socioeconomic positions leave their communities with relatively little internal structural differentiation, because of high geographic mobility, and because the members of the new Spanish-speaking working class are often in temporary and contingent occupations, their social networks generally create only limited formal institutions and they often do not, as networks, take control of institutions. As noted in the discussion of Latino community development corporations, organizations such as CDCs tend to be directed toward seeking external financial and social investments. The religious institutions that so many researchers have found to be central foci for these immigrants remain structures that seek to act on the immigrants, rather than formalizations of their own interpersonal relations.

Manago (2007) found that the day labor activities of the immigrants she studied reinforced their impermanence in American society, so that their religious gatherings provided mutual psychological support, but did not mobilize them for utilizing cooperation for upward mobility. The various Protestant and Catholic missions in their social functions continue to operate as service providers, bringing assistance to the immigrant communities, rather than as foci for community network activities. While important for collective identity and psychological support, these institutions tend not to be locations for turning interpersonal relations into assets.

At this point, it is important to emphasize that this description of why immigrant networks can result in weak institutions is not a statement of destiny. It is possible that as the settlements in new destinations become more established over time, communities may develop stronger institutions. To achieve a greater understanding of what I have called "strong institutions," though, I will turn now to examples of some of the stronger formal institutions and discuss the role of social networks in creating and maintaining these. Given the centrality of religious institutions for mobilizing the resources of immigrant networks, I will look first in greater depth at religion as a source of social capital.

Religion as Organization: Faith and Social Capital

Robert Bellah (1970) has argued that religion is a central source of group identity and motivation for individuals. Along these lines, network researchers have found support for the Durkheimian argument that integration in a network of co-religionists protects individuals against anomie (Brashears, 2010). Accordingly, one should expect that the religious affiliation and participation of immigrants should constitute an important aspect of relations within a group and that social connections based on religious institutions should influence how immigrants adjust to the world around them.

Religious institutions exist in networks of social relations and provide these networks with foci of the sort described by Scott Feld (1981). Church or temple membership is a prime source of identity and motivation precisely because it is a focus for organizing the social relations of a group. First-generation immigrants perceive it as the one real element of continuity between their country of origin and their new homeland and as an effective strategy for linking themselves with their American-born or -reared children while acquiring acceptance in the host society (Williams, 1988).

Social scientific literature on the post-1965 immigrants generally portrays religious institutions as important for immigrant networks and as mostly enabling in character. In the edited volume *Religion and the New Immigrants* (2000), Ebaugh and Chafetz bring together 13 case studies of a wide range of immigrant religions in Houston, Texas, where immigrants made up nearly a quarter of the population at the time of publication. In their discussion of thematic issues, the editors point out that these widely varying faith-based organizations serve as community centers and that they tend to take on the participatory, congregational structure identified by R. Stephen Warner (1994).

Among post-1965 immigrant religious institutions, Korean churches may have drawn the most attention as foci of immigrant network activity. Pyong Gap Min, probably the foremost authority on Korean immigrants, noted in an article published in 1992 that the vast majority of Korean immigrants in the United States were associated with ethnic churches. Min identified four social functions of these churches: they provided fellowship for Korean immigrants, they maintained Korean cultural traditions, they provided social services for church members and for the Korean community as a whole, and they provided social status and positions for Korean immigrants. Korean churches, in other words, act as centers that connect immigrants to other immigrants, maintain identification with the homeland and the group, create a structured society, and mobilize immigrants to contribute to mutual assistance.

As network foci, Korean churches concentrate the flow of information and resources available in Korean immigrant communities. For example, in a case study of a Korean congregation in Houston, Kwon (1997) found that the church brought entrepreneurs together with potential customers and employees, and was a place where new immigrants could find work. In a co-authored article on the functions of the Korean church for entrepreneurship, Kwon, Ebaugh, and Hagan (1997) described how the cell group ministry, a common organizational form within Korean churches, established a social structure within Korean immigrant communities and made social relations a basis for the central economic activity of Koreans: small-scale self-employment. "Most of the services that the Korean Church provides to help recent immigrants adapt to their new environment," these authors write, "are provided informally through interpersonal connections among members of the church. The cell group ministry within the church constitutes the structural network system that serves as the infrastructure for informal personal connections" (p. 249). The cells are small groups established on a geographical basis under larger divisions. The gatherings of cell members "serve as the backbone of an informal network that assists immigrants in meeting the social, economic, cultural, and religious challenges faced by new immigrants in the settlement process" (p. 250). The cell group structure is an example of the organization of informal networks into formal patterns on the basis of a religious institution as a focus.

Although Korean churches are not intended for economic networking, they often have that function. In my own work on social networks in Southeast Asian communities, I have found that religious organizations frequently emerge as central social connectors within immigrant ethnic enclaves. In a manner similar to that in the Korean congregation studied by Kwon and her co-authors, the religious institution in my Vietnamese community case study with Min Zhou came into existence as a critical part of the formal infrastructure of informal personal relations. "As in Little Saigon [in Orange County]," we observed, "the structures of Versailles Village became more formally institutionalized over time. In the beginning, the community was largely maintained by the informal networks of families and friends. As time went on, existing formal organizations were consolidated and new organizations were established. The Catholic church was the most important of the various organizations" (Zhou and Bankston, 1998: 81).

The Vietnamese Catholic church, we noted, was at the center of this community not only socially but even geographically. Since our interest was primarily the adaptation of young people, we concentrated on how the church served as a primary mechanism for integrating them into the community's system of ethnic relations. But the church has also been the institutional basis for mobilizing the institutional relations of adults. It is the location where other formal institutions interlock, a topic that will be discussed further in the following section. Because it is where people come together, it has the latent function of coordinating economic activities, as in the Korean example. Twice in the community's history, it served as the structural basis for political organization when New Orleans business and governmental leaders planned to place a potentially hazardous landfill next to the neighborhood (Bankston, 1990; Vu et al., 2009). Following the devastation of the area by Hurricane Katrina, neighbors met at the church to coordinate their mutual assistance in rebuilding (Vu et al., 2009).

Religious institutions do not influence every aspect of immigrant social relations in every immigrant community to the extent that the church does in this one. Still, Min Zhou and I (1998: 98) pointed out that religious institutions such as the Buddhist temple in New York City and the Buddhist community center in Orange County's Little Saigon are also coordinating points for social functions among non-Catholic Vietnamese. Along these lines, Paul J. Rutledge (1985) found that Vietnamese community social relations in Oklahoma City revolved around religious institutions. While immigrant networks can be purely secular in character, because religion is such a fundamental source of collective identity and mobilization, tightly interconnected immigrant networks often do manifest themselves as religious institutions, which in turn provide an explicit structure for informal interpersonal relations.

Chapter 5 discussed variants on physical communities as geographic manifestations of network relationships. One can also see a geographical dimension to the role of religious institutions as key network foci. In the Korean example, in which Korean immigrants did not live in a single neighborhood, the church maintained an ethnic network through cell groups in different residential areas that linked ethnic social relations together in a single church congregation. In the Vietnamese example, the church was located at the geographic center as well as the social center of a residential enclave. An example of another immigrant settlement, of Lao in small town and rural southern Louisiana, can give some insight into yet another geographical variation on the functioning of a religious institution within an immigrant social network.

The Lao began moving to Iberia Parish in Louisiana in the early 1980s, seeking job opportunities. At that time the Federal Comprehensive Employment and Training Act (CETA) had provided funding for training in pipe-fitting, welding, and related skills in demand in the region. When a few Lao found this training, and the jobs that followed it, word of available employment spread through the Lao family and friendship networks and others began moving to the region. They settled where there were homes available, establishing a first enclave in Section 8 housing in a lower-income area of New Iberia. As their jobs began providing them with income, they started to move out of this location. However, there were insufficient homes available for all of them in any single neighborhood, so they settled as small clusters of families throughout local suburbs (Bankston, 1996; 1997; 2000; Zhou et al., 2001).

By 1986, they had acquired enough of a shared financial basis to plan their own community and cultural center. In that year, a number of men generally recognized as leaders, often because they were former military officers (again, this shows the importance of internal differentiation and authority structures for an immigrant network), formed the Temple Corporation, an association dedicated to building a Lao-style Buddhist temple that would be surrounded by an ethnic residential enclave. Because insufficient space was available within the confines of the city of New Iberia, the Temple Corporation, by pooling funds from the immigrant community, purchased land in a sparsely populated rural area to the north of the town.

By 1987, the temple was completed and streets named after places in Laos were set out in front of it. During the early 1990s, the temple village began to run out of room for new households and local Lao began to establish homes on a stretch of land a little under a quarter of a mile to the west of the temple. In addition to space considerations, though, the geographical structure of the Lao community was affected by the fact that anyone who wanted to live within the physical ethnic concentration around the temple had to build a home, rather than purchase an existing one. The geographic arrangement therefore became a heavily concentrated enclave around the temple, with lines of social connection extending out to the clusters of suburban homes that had radiated outward from the initial enclave in low-income housing in New Iberia (Bankston, 1996; 1997).

By linking those living in the concentrated settlements around the temple and those in the suburban clusters, the temple not only enabled the local Lao to interact and support each other, but also became the place where bridging ties linked the community to opportunities in the larger society. When I interviewed the human resources director of one of the large companies building offshore oil structures where he found his many skilled Lao craft workers, he told me, "one of our foremen is the financial manager at that Buddhist whatchamacallit [i.e., temple] . . . People go to him for a job and he just refers them here" (Zhou et al., 2001: 465). The financial manager, through the network centrality formalized by his position and his authority within the network and his position outside the network, could serve as a critical conduit of information.

The temple even provided a location for critical bridging ties that enabled the creation of the physical Lao community. An adult daughter of one of the lay leaders of the temple community was employed by a local bank as a loan officer in charge of mortgages. Most of the homes around the temple and many of those in the suburban clusters were financed by this bank with her assistance. Her own home was located in the temple community and she frequently met with customers on or near the temple grounds (Bankston, 1997; Zhou et al., 2001).

Religious institutions, then, are frequently key foci for immigrant networks and can facilitate the transformation of a web of social ties into assets when the institutions arise directly from interpersonal relations and serve as means for action through networks. The de facto congregational structure of many immigrant religious institutions can be seen as a reflection of informal immigrant networks taking shape and working within formal structures. Immigrant religious institutions can contribute to turning networks into social capital through their latent functions of channeling economic information and resources. Churches, temples, or other places of spiritual expression exist within the geographic structure of immigrant communities, and connect people spatially in ways that depend on that geography. While religion is often central as a formal network institution, though, immigrant communities, especially those that most effectively turn social relations into assets, entail other organizations and associations. The next section turns to the question of how all of these may connect and work together.

Interlocking Institutions

In *Growing Up American* (1998), Min Zhou and I noted that Vietnamese American communities gave rise to numerous secular social organizations that were often closely connected to a central religious organization. In the community of our case study, we noted that the formal organizations included, among others, the Vietnamese American Voters' Association, the Political Prisoner Veterans Union, the Versailles Neighborhood Association, the *Dung Lac* youth program, and the Vietnamese Educational Association. All of these different formal institutions provided means of structuring network activities. For example, the Voters' Association provided citizenship classes, information on public issues, and the basis for mobilizing in the political activities that immediately concerned the city. The Neighborhood Association was concerned with security and upkeep. The Educational Association ran afternoon classes at a child development center.

One way in which these organizations interlock is through overlapping membership. There is, then, a densely interconnected institutional network that can be seen as the formalization of a densely interconnected interpersonal network. The institutions are more than foci of interpersonal networks; they are the means by which the interpersonal networks achieve explicitly recognized goals, and their capacity for achieving these goals is enhanced by organizational collaboration. In fact, the entire community has a formal structure. It is divided into zones, each of which has a zone leader who represents it at meetings to decide on community activities and policies.

Interlocking formal institutions are also important for turning interpersonal relations into social capital for groups in communities that do not show such an enclave-type character. Caroline B. Brettell (2005) has found that multiple, interlocking institutions were essential sources of social capital for South Asians in the Dallas–Fort Worth metroplex. She noted that "the organizations that primarily nurture the development and deployment of bonding social capital are religious and regional [i.e., based on regions of origin in South Asia]" (p. 858). The regional associations provided social contacts based on the sense of shared place of origin and enabled association members to maintain these contacts among their children. The social contacts enabled the South Asian immigrants "to develop a close network of people of similar cultural background with whom one can interact on a regular basis and whom one can trust as one would one's own family or people one had known for some time. This element of trust has often been described as a key component of social capital" (p. 859). These regional associations, based on voluntary membership with elected boards of directors, typically ran a variety of programs (including charitable fund raising, language classes, youth camps, and programs for elders) through committee structures – a system of institutional structures within institutions.

The regional associations, further, linked those in the local community to wider national networks based on region of origin. "Regional associations," Brettell observed, "are often networked into nationwide umbrella associations (for example, of all the Gujarati associations in the US or all the Kerala associations in the US)" (2005: 859). The regional associations were linked to religious institutions, chiefly Hindu temples, that brought together the region-of-origin groups.

Brettell's South Asian example of interlocking institutions reveals another aspect of immigrant ethnicity: the tendency of settlement in a new location to reshape ideas of ethnicity and create new kinds of immigrant ethnic networks. Brettell has observed that the temples express a general Hindu identity that is broader than that of the regional associations. The emergence of Pan-Southeast Asian and Pan-Asian identities also finds expression in new kinds of ties, through organizations such as the India Association of North Texas and the Asian Chamber of Commerce. The origins and processes that lead beyond specific ethnic organizations and toward broader pan-ethnic entities pose issues for greater research regarding the emergence of new organizational networks. At present, one can observe that the regional associations, as sources of bonding ties, provided structures for the networks in which individuals were the most immediately connected, and the wider institutional structures integrated these into formal systems of bridging ties.

Networks and Symbolic Associations

In an influential paper published in 1979, Herbert Gans argued that American ethnic groups derived from immigration were reaching a stage of acculturation in which ethnic identification was primarily a matter of consumption of ethnic symbols detached from actual social ties to other group members. Ethnicity may become symbolic in character because members of a group retain some sense of identification after group members have moved out of a residential concentration, or they may move away because their identification has become purely symbolic in character. There has indeed been a tendency for ethnicity to become largely symbolic for many descendants of earlier ethnic groups. However, insofar as ethnicity is a basis for engaging in interpersonal relations, the symbolism produced by the sense of membership can maintain networks as functional interpersonal webs. The regional associations described by Brettell (2005), for example, derive from individuals' sense of symbolic identification with a heritage, but the symbolic attachment has meaningful consequences for social linkages to the group. The very fact that many of the respondents in her study did not live together in an ethnic residential enclave made formal institutions created out of the sense of cultural identification particularly useful as network foci. One of her respondents described the meetings of the regional associations as "a good way to start looking for potential spouses for your children because all of the people are from the same background" (p. 860). The tendency of many Asian Indians not to live in ethnically concentrated areas was precisely what made these associations so valuable for maintaining social ties and forming kinship links: "Doing this [looking for spouses for adult offspring] in India is so much easier because everyone knows everyone . . . But in the United States you are often working in a vacuum because neighbors do not know one another. There are not the kind of powerful connections that exist in India so it is much harder to get information" (p. 860).

Formal organizations, such as these regional associations, make and maintain ties among people by serving as symbolic representations of group identity. There is a symbolic side to most immigrant-based organizations. The Vietnamese Voters' Association and the Vietnamese Educational Association do not just serve civic and educational goals; they also serve the goals of people who are bound together by common cultural symbolism.

However, these organizations are only secondarily symbolic in character. For members of immigrant groups who are not living surrounded by co-ethnics, though, organizations that have the primary purpose of symbolizing ethnicity can be critical to maintaining immigrant networks; that is, transforming categories into "catnets."

To draw again on the Filipino example, in Chapter 5 I discussed the informal ties maintained through get-togethers and efforts to make contact with newly arrived immigrants. These informal networks are supported by a wide variety of organizations and clubs that affirm and express their ethnic identities. On this issue, Posadas (1999: 60) remarks that "an exhaustive examination of organizations and associations created by Filipino Americans would be a monumental, if not an impossible task." Posadas (pp. 60–1) observes that "as officers and members of innumerable associations, Filipino Americans define and re-define attachments outside of their family networks."

Along with festivals and picnics, one of the prominent activities of Filipino clubs in the United States is the holding of beauty pageants, a symbolic reminder of life in the Philippines, where this type of event is common. Beauty pageants serve to raise funds for community organizations and to reinforce ethnic identity and solidarity. On the financial importance of Filipino beauty pageants in the U.S., one newspaper reporter wrote that in southern California alone "these pageants raise . . . thousands of dollars each year" (Bonus, 2000: 121).

The symbolically rich activities of these organizations can clearly turn social relations based on immigrant ethnicity into financial capital. But they also bring people together around shared ethic identification and thereby reinforce the informal relations. Symbolic associations create social ties.

In examining the role of formal institutions as network foci, I have argued that the capacity of formal institutions to transform interpersonal relations into assets depends on how closely bound the institutions are to underlying social networks and on the ability of those networks to act through formal institutions. I have identified religious organizations as especially important network foci, and discussed the role of interlocking formal institutions for enabling group action. Finally, I have suggested that symbolic associations and organizations help to maintain interpersonal relations on the basis of shared immigrant backgrounds, and this kind of symbolic institutional focus can be especially useful in mobilizing groups that do not live in enclave-type situations. This discussion of goals and assets raises questions, though. What goal-directed activities do immigrant groups engage in? If interpersonal relations among immigrants may be "capital," where is the capital invested? To answer these questions, Chapters 7 and 8 will consider how network relations among immigrant group members may "pay off" through shaping economic adaptation among adults and educational adaptation among children.

7

Adaptation: Employment and the Economy

The idea that people find economic opportunities through network ties is well established, even though there has long been debate about what kinds of ties lead to opportunities under differing circumstances. The "strength of weak ties" argument, for instance, suggests that the best opportunities may come from having information beyond a single social circle, so that upward mobility is most likely for those who have access to wide-ranging contacts. Among immigrants, having links to people outside an immigrant social circle can often be a source of opportunities. Professionals who find their occupations because they know others in purely professional circles, for example, may enjoy economic advantages that are in no way dependent on their co-ethnics. Laborers may find jobs through non-immigrant recruiters.

Although occupations and jobs do not necessarily come from any network connections, some kind of network is usually involved in letting job seekers know where to look. Still, the social contacts who provide information may all be non-immigrants. Even when immigrants are vastly overrepresented in an occupational field, it is not logically necessary that this be a result of immigrant social networks. Even when there is no logical necessity that immigrant networks be involved, though, in practice they often are. While the larger structural forces discussed in Chapter 3 may lie behind immigrant occupational specialization, this specialization creates relevant immigrant networks. The concentration of women from the Philippines in nursing not only means that those who go into this profession have greater chances of migrating, it means that women deciding on a career path know other women who have gone into this line of work and migrated, so that occupational decisions have been shaped by interpersonal connections within the broader contexts of labor demand in the United States and educational institutions in the Philippines. After arriving in the United States and taking up a job in a hospital, ethnic specialization means that the workplace will be a location for forming ethnically based social circles. Moreover, the specialization means that at those symbolic associations that I examined in the last section of Chapter 6 there will be many contacts with people who work in hospitals and know about new openings.

Immigrant networks are also relevant for laborers who find jobs through non-immigrant recruiters. Immigrants who know the recruiters will put those agents of employers in touch with other immigrants seeking work and they will provide information about available work to others within their social circles. Thus, an immigrant occupational niche arises because of the contextual setting in the labor market, such as a demand for low-wage, highly mobile workers or a demand for skills available in another country but in short supply in the United States or among non-immigrants. In the case of the skilled Lao workers in offshore oil structures (see the section on religion as organization in Chapter 6), a shortage of native-born workers opened spaces that could be occupied by immigrants (on this issue, see also Donato and Bankston, 2008). But in order for immigrants to fill those spaces, there had to be ways for employers to find immigrant workers and for workers to find employers. In that Lao example, the demand for welders, pipe-fitters, and related occupations led to the establishment of a government training program. Information about the program reached Lao job seekers, whose interpersonal networks began to pull in more Lao workers. As Lao entered these jobs in larger numbers, they began to train each other, and the jobs increased as ethnic concentrations even after the government program ended (Bankston, 1997).

Immigrant occupational specializations, conceived of as results of interpersonal contacts acting within labor market contexts, involve both binding ties and bridging ties, and enabling and constraining social relations. The social bonds among the Lao led them to share information about jobs in Louisiana within ethnic networks and to share skills. These bonds would have been useless, though, without connecting individuals acting as bridges. The pioneers who first learned about the CETA training had to make contacts outside of their own group in order to bring in the information. After this work became a Lao specialization, the company foreman who was also a temple official was a bridge between the company and those within the immigrant social circle.

Clearly, having access to jobs through contacts within a network and through bridges to opportunities can be seen as enabling in nature. Every channel of access is also a constraint, though. The more the Lao were concentrated in building offshore structures, the more their social ties directed them toward jobs in that industry and away from other kinds of jobs. Having developed bridges with job providers in one field leads to greater concentration on those specific bridges.

This general process of network channeling within labor market contexts takes place across immigrant and other ethnic groups. The extent to which the constraint side of the channeling, as opposed to the enabling side, is evident depends in large part on the relative desirability of the occupational concentration (although network constraints without adequate bridges may be even more problematic, since this situation results in high unemployment or low labor force participation). Initial movements of an immigrant group into an occupational specialization may result from skills cultivated in the home country (see Chapter 3 and Figure 3.1). At approximately the same time that the Lao were moving into construction of structures for offshore oil production, for example, Mexican immigrants were becoming a notable presence in similar jobs because of the skills acquired in Mexico due to that country's active petroleum production (Donato et al., 2001). The initial movements may also owe a great deal to historical accident, as was the case among the Lao workers. However, once the channeling has begun, networks tend to direct more and more workers of specific immigrant ethnicities toward specific jobs, resulting in immigrant jobs – jobs in which workers of particular immigrant backgrounds are concentrated.

One way in which social relations can become assets for immigrants, then, is through linking immigrants to job opportunities. This tends to create immigrant occupational niches. There is, though, another way that social relations among immigrants can lead to opportunities and create immigrant specializations. Interpersonal relations can also create opportunities for immigrants by supporting and encouraging entrepreneurship and jobs within or connected to businesses created through ties among immigrants. Light et al. (1999) argued that much of existing network theory tended to focus exclusively on locating existing opportunities, but that immigrants could also create opportunities, through entrepreneurship based on ethnic social relations. "When immigrant networks support co-ethnic entrepreneurship, thus creating an ethnic economy, they expand the existing economy in the destination locality" (Light et al., 1999: 10).

Entrepreneurship based on social relations among immigrants often takes the form of providing goods or services in demand in one's own ethnic group. The classic example of this is restaurants. Wherever there are large numbers of Chinese or Cuban immigrants there is a demand for Chinese or Cuban food, and no one can provide this food better than Chinese or Cuban restaurateurs. In my observations of the Greater New Orleans area, I have noted that the influx of Mexican and Central American construction workers following Hurricane Katrina in late 2005 was followed almost immediately by a flowering of Latin American eateries around the settlement locations (Bankston, 2009a). Many of these establishments very quickly grew in popularity among the native-born population, a common occurrence historically among ethnic restaurants. Thus, although ethnic immigrant businesses may have connections to group members as an initial asset, for broader success the business owners need to make bridges to larger sets of customers.

Like ethnic jobs in general, immigrant ethnic business specializations can result from information and direction provided along network lines. In recounting how Asian Indians from Gujarat came to dominate the American motel industry, Pawan Dhingra tells us that the occupational specialization can be traced back to the 1940s when an undocumented Gujarati immigrant in San Francisco managed to buy a hotel that had been owned by a Japanese who had been forced into an internment camp (Dhingra, 2012: 50). "As a fellow Gujarati, Desai most likely attracted the Gujarati immigrant laborers of the 1940s and 1950s who needed to stay in residential hotels when in San Francisco. Staying at Desai's hotel created a link for them to jobs in the industry" (p. 54). From this beginning, Gujaratis shifted from hotels to motels. The first motel owned by a member of the immigrant group was also in San Francisco, in the early 1960s. As more Gujaratis and other Indians arrived in the 1960s and 1970s, they faced low-wage jobs and discrimination in the larger labor market, but also opportunities to work for relatives or other co-ethnics who owned hotels. As in other cases of network channeling, the more Gujaratis who found work in hotels, the stronger the network direction to those jobs became and working toward ownership of motels became the chief route for upward mobility.

Two of the ways in which relations among immigrants can build an economic specialization, then, are through network channeling toward opportunities and through immigrant economic activities providing jobs to other immigrants. Further, the employment relationship can itself be transformed into human capital: working for Asian Indian motel owners enables Asian Indian employees to learn the skills to run their own hotels. On the other side, co-ethnic employees, most often extended family members, have provided low-wage labor to owners, making immigrant interpersonal relationships a source of financial capital by generating savings in salaries. "In addition," Dhingra tells us, "the free accommodations to sponsored relatives helped them save enough money to possibly buy their own establishments [even at low wage levels]" (2012: 71). Further, those purchasing motels "borrowed money from relatives and close friends. Because the lenders know how to run motels, they felt comfortable lending money based on a handshake to someone buying a motel. It was not uncommon for twenty or more people to lend $2,000 each" (p. 77).

The motel example illustrates why one can go beyond speaking of immigrant ethnic jobs as consequences of network channeling within labor markets to speak of immigrant ethnic economies as network phenomena. In the latter, relations among immigrants do more than direct individuals toward occupational specializations. The interpersonal relations create an entire set of economic inter-actions, such as guaranteed jobs, low-cost labor, means of capital accumulation, and sources of credit for investment.

The ethnic enclave economy described by Alejandro Portes (1987) was an especially self-contained variety of ethnic economy, in which economic activities took place in an immigrant residential enclave and involved relationships among immigrant ethnic employers, employees, and (at least initially) customers within that residential enclave. Even that enclave economy was not completely self-contained, though. As Cuban businesses in south Florida flourished, they increasingly served customers who were not members of the Cuban community, and these businesses spread and invested outside of this community.

In the Gujarati motel example, Dhingra (2012) tells us that the motel owners began as "middleman minorities," specializing in low-cost motels serving mainly low-income members of native-born minorities. Immigrant networks provided the entrepreneurs, the labor, and the capital. Native-born minorities provided the customers. Later, many of the motel owners moved upscale, but they were still serving customers almost entirely outside their own group.

Another variation on the linkages between network-based immigrant ethnic economies and outsiders can occur when the immigrant network supplies the information about opportunities, the skills, and the capital, and some set of outsiders supplies at least part of the labor. This situation brings up one of the most interesting ways in which immigrant networks as means of economic adaptation can shape ethnic stratification. Since networks direct people toward ethnic jobs, economic relations can generally be seen as networks of networks, as ways in which occupational specializations connect. Before looking at economic linkages across immigrant networks, though, it will be useful to examine the occupations containing the largest numbers of immigrants and to consider the role of networks in directing individuals toward these occupations.

Ethnic Jobs: America's Immigrant Working Class

The large number of undocumented immigrants makes most calculations of immigrant characteristics tentative, but data from the American Community Survey (ACS) of 2011 can give us some idea of immigrant occupational specialization. Among workers born in Mexico, the sending country of the largest number of immigrants, 14.1 percent were in construction and 10.2 percent were in eating and drinking places, so that one-fourth of all Mexican immigrants were in just these two industries. An additional 8.3 percent worked in agricultural production and 4.2 percent were in landscape and horticultural services.

The most common occupations among Mexican-born workers were (in order): farm workers, cooks, housekeepers and maids, gardeners and groundskeepers, construction laborers, janitors, truck and delivery drivers, laborers outside construction, unclassified machine operators, carpenters, cashiers, food preparation workers, nursing aides and attendants, hand packers and packagers, painters in construction and maintenance, and assemblers of electrical equipment. Together, these working-class occupations held a majority of Mexican-born workers in the United States, although a precise counting of undocumented workers would probably have placed even more in jobs such as farm workers, groundskeepers, and construction laborers (Ruggles et al., 2010).

Immigrants from Mexico made up about 5 percent of the total American labor force. This was a large proportion for arrivals from a single nation, but Mexicans made up even greater percentages of some occupational categories. Over one-fifth of all the gardeners and groundskeepers in the United States in the 2011 ACS were Mexican immigrants. Mexican immigrants also made up over one-third of all farm workers and nearly half of all American graders and sorters of agricultural products. They were well over one-fourth of all drywall installers, a third of all plasterers, and over one-fifth of all concrete and cement workers and of all roofers and slaters. Close to a fifth of American butchers and meat-cutters and over one-fifth of hand packers and packagers were Mexican immigrants (Ruggles et al., 2010). This is a portrait of an immigrant group that is not only highly concentrated in lower-level manual work, but constitutes a major part of the workforce in manual labor.

The Spanish-speaking working class, primarily of Mexican origin, was not only prevalent in these occupational groups in the United States; it was also both much larger in sheer size and wider spread across the American nation than ever before. The economic restructuring and rise of new industries discussed in Chapter 3 provided the context for these developments. The transformation of the meat-packing industry from skilled craft workers in urban areas to unskilled laborers in rural regions and small towns, for example, created a context of demand for a new force of relatively low-paid employees who were willing to relocate. As Hirschman and Massey note, though, "[p]eople can only respond to the various pushes and pulls if they are aware of them; and individuals are not wholly independent actors, but are constrained by information about opportunities in distant locations. Social ties embedded within migrant networks can provide this information and lower the costs of migration" (Hirschman and Massey, 2008: 4–5).

As social networks channel individuals to new geographic locations, they channel them to new occupational locations. Pioneers move to places to take up occupational opportunities, and their network contacts follow them both to the locations and to the workplaces. Through cumulative causation, once a flow has begun, to a place and an occupational specialization, jobs take in ever greater numbers of immigrants until the jobs become closely associated with immigrant ethnicity. The movement along network channels will also occur within a geographic location that has become home to a substantial immigrant population.

In my own studies of the growth of a Latino working class in the New Orleans area, I have found that immigrant arrivals were encouraged by a demand for construction workers in such lower-level positions as drywall installers and roofers (Sisk and Bankston, 2012). Even after the work of reconstruction slowed, workers found other types of jobs, including miscellaneous manual labor and lawn care, and workers with whom they had ties followed them into these jobs (Bankston, 2009a; 2012a). The cumulative causation effect of networked immigration was increasing the size of the worker population and also moving them into a wider range of work activities, in the process broadening their networks.

One extremely helpful study of the relationship between networks and the macroeconomic context of the developing new immigrant working class, by Maria de Lourdes Villar (1992), examined changes in networks in the Chicago area. During the late 1960s, employers in the area began seeking to cut their labor costs by hiring Mexican workers and by encouraging these workers to bring in others, often paying bonuses for recruitment. These workers, of course, brought in other Mexicans, beginning with members of their own households. By the late 1970s, employers no longer needed to offer monetary incentives. They could rely on their Mexican workers to recruit through kinship networks. Because they could bring in new employees and communicate with them effectively, trusted immigrants often became senior employees, acting as bridges between companies and workers. By the late 1980s, the flow of new arrivals expanded beyond relatively closed network circles, and the senior immigrant workers began hiring workers through weaker ties to workers who might be friends of acquaintances. Often these senior workers took bribes or charged fees to these newer workers, who could then bring in people in their own social circles. Thus, the networks continued to be based on immigrant ethnicity, but the expansion of the labor force weakened the linkages in a manner consistent with the description of new Mexican immigrant communities that I offered in Chapter 5 in the section on neighborhoods and networks in the Spanish-speaking working class.

While immigrant ethnic jobs tend to remain within stratification levels, because of the intertwined influences of contextual demand and network channeling, they do often tend to diversify as an immigrant population grows and includes more interpersonal networks. Despite the relative lack of stratification among large segments of the Latino immigrant population, some of the ethnic jobs performed by the Spanish-speaking working class of North America may entail self-employment and entrepreneurship, especially in the informal sector. In the brief description of Mexican immigrant occupational concentrations at the start of this section, I pointed out that Census evidence indicates that Mexican immigrants constitute about one-fifth of all U.S. gardeners and groundskeepers. In fact, the openness of work such as lawn care to undocumented workers probably means that Mexican immigrants make up an even larger proportion of this type of labor. Alvaro Huerta (2007), looking at immigrant gardeners in Los Angeles, has described a network-driven economic strategy that in many respects resembles immigrant entrepreneurship among other groups. According to Huerta, immigrants from Mexico often turn to lawn care to generate opportunities that are not available to them in the larger economy. Jobs in lawn care involve *patrons*, or bosses, who own equipment such as lawnmowers and trimmers and make arrangements with clients, and *trabajadores*, or workers.

> [P]aid gardeners predominantly rely on their social networks to navigate the informal economy. Instead of accessing classified ads to meet his labor needs, the patron typically resorts to strong ties like an extended family network, friends, neighbors, colleagues, and individuals from the same hometown to hire a trabajador. This situation not only saves the patron time and money, but it also provides him with a trustworthy and loyal workforce. By hiring his sibling or brother-in-law, the patron does not have to be constantly worried about the trabajador stealing his equipment or clients. (Huerta, 2007: 15)

Here, it should be noted that although the *patrons* are self-employed in the sense that they own their own machinery and hire their own workers, they are essentially performing contract labor. The *patrons* do have bosses: all of the people who hire them to do yard work. The householders in Los Angeles may derive direct economic benefits from the relatively low-cost labor of immigrant gardeners, but the householders also receive benefits generated from the network connections of the *patrons*. Lawn maintenance can be done by a team of workers and that team is put together by a single individual with whom the householders make arrangements. The *patron* is a crucial bridging central connector who can create jobs for members of his social circle, but also provides a ready-made workforce to a circle of people looking for lawn care.

Ramirez and Hondagneu-Sotelo (2009) have found that the lawn care business, providing services to suburban homeowners, combines elements of ethnic entrepreneurship and subjugated service work. They suggest that this type of contract labor on the part of mainly immigrant men is analogous in many respects to the involvement of immigrant women in domestic labor, but that it is part of a trend toward hybrid entrepreneurship and service work. While there is some occupational differentiation and upward mobility within these hybrids, both the differentiation and mobility are extremely limited.

There are clear parallels between *patrons* hiring friends and relatives to do lawn work and immigrant senior employees in companies drawing on immigrant networks to find workers. In both cases, immigrants who have acquired some experience and made contact with outside employers act as connectors, with clear advantages for the outsiders. Employers may be corporations or they may be individuals, but in either case they are sets of people seeking to find others to perform certain jobs. The costs of labor for recruiters consist of finding workers, organizing them, and (in many cases) training them. The immigrant network absorbs all of these costs. Householders with yards to be maintained need only meet someone with a crew, and this is usually done by word of mouth among social circles of householders. Managers of companies need only find immigrant foremen with access to co-ethnics, and the networks of the foremen find and organize the workers, and often train them.

On this last point, Nestor Rodriguez (2004) has observed that employers are not motivated only by the search for low-cost labor in hiring immigrant workers. In fact, Rodriguez remarked, employers are often willing to pay their immigrant workers a prevailing wage or at least the federal minimum wage, if the employers can secure another major advantage. "The advantage," he writes

> is acquiring a self-regulating and self-sustaining labor supply, that is, a labor supply that is self-recruiting, self-training, and self-disciplining ... The arrangement is similar to the benefits of out-sourcing work, but without actually having to contract with an external firm. The employer simply turns over the responsibilities of the labor process to the immigrant workforce, whose members organize and operate the work process through internal social networks and hierarchies ... The end result is that the employer saves on the cost of managing and maintaining a labor force, as the labor cost is reduced mainly to paying for work performed. (Rodriguez, 2004: 454–5)

Networks provide assets for immigrants, but the kinds of assets they can provide depend on the resources and information available through immigrant social ties. Immigrant networks also provide assets (or social capital) for outside groups, though, such as corporate or individual employers. The assets move in both directions through individuals who act as connectors. Seen in this way, ethnic stratification, that is, the tendency of immigrant and other ethnic groups to concentrate at identifiable socioeconomic levels, is not a matter solely of individual immigration and labor demand or even only of migration networks enabling individuals to move in search of jobs. It is a matter of interactions among immigrants creating a workforce that serves the interests of employers and of individuals serving as bridges between the two. The kind of labor arrangement that can provide readily available construction workers to contractors can also provide lawn care workers to householders, and the arrangement that can provide labor for poultry preparation can provide labor for carpet manufacture. Human capital, the possession of skills, may often be important, but even that can be created by immigrant networks within the process of finding employment, since workers can train each other. As immigrant networks connect to particular sets of employers, the interactions among immigrants reinforce their specialization in types of work.

This network reinforcement of immigrant ethnic specialization is not peculiar to the large Spanish-speaking working class, but occurs across groups. Dhingra (2012), in the work cited in the previous section, noted that young Gujaratis who are planning to migrate to the United States often do not pursue higher education, unlike many other South Asian groups. This is because their social ties channel them toward work in the hospitality industry, and the potential immigrants often see higher education not only as a distraction, but as an actual disadvantage. Again, in this example, the social network can be transformed into human capital (motel experience) that trains people in ways that yield benefits for outsiders (businesses that supply motels, as well as customers), with little or no cost to the outsiders.

Before looking further at ethnic specialization and social capital across groups, it should be noted that the arrangement of social ties within a stratification level does vary. In the Los Angeles immigrant gardening example (Huerta, 2007), the *patron*'s ability to run a lawn care service depends on strong ties, on close relations to kin or friends, since the service runs on trust. Lawn care services are small operations, though, and trust is a matter of the kind of repeated interaction inconsistent with high mobility. While this type of activity is certainly part of the immigrant labor market, high geographic mobility, employment in large workplaces, and the sheer size of the immigrant population (especially the Mexican-origin population) tend to place more emphasis on less close-knit ties. In Villar's (1992) case study in Chicago, we saw that as immigrant recruiting networks included more people, they tended to rely more on weak ties (and less trust) among individuals.

Social Capital and Ethnic Specialization

Networks respond to economic settings, but they also perpetuate those settings. Immigrants from Latin America respond to the demand for labor in construction or in restructuring and relocating industries, but as they respond their social networks become focused on work in those occupational areas, and ethnic specialization intensifies through cumulative causation. In the case of immigrant jobs, the social capital within an immigrant group is largely a matter of social relations providing help in finding opportunities. Since the opportunities are those to which the immigrants have access, social capital promotes ethnic specialization.

The occupational specialization through network channeling can occur in entrepreneurial activities, as well. In the classic case of the immigrant ethnic economy, the growth of immigration itself can provide an economic context. Immigrant businesses often begin by serving the needs of co-ethnics. Even in this case, though, successful businesses grow beyond immigrant customers. Cuban or Chinese restaurants begin to serve customers outside their ethnic groups. But immigrant entrepreneurial activities can also begin by selling goods or services to outside customers. A demand for business products, such as shops in underserved neighborhoods or hospitality services that native-born Americans need but are reluctant to supply, creates an opening for entrepreneurs. In the case of ethnic economies, though, whether they primarily serve co-ethnics or outsiders, social capital consists of creating opportunities, as well as directing people to them. Immigrant social relations can become a way of generating financial capital, through access to loans and low-cost labor provided by ethnic groups, and of generating human capital, through on-the-job training for entrepreneurship.

In Chapter 8, I will examine how social relations within immigrant groups may sometimes dissolve ethnic specialization over the course of generations, mainly by promoting upward mobility through schooling. Within first generations, though, the network channeling of individuals and the creation of assets by ethnic networks tend to position immigrants at specific places in the system of socioeconomic stratification. Some immigrant groups specialize as laborers, others as shop-keepers, others as motel owners, and still others as owners of garment factories. In keeping with the idea of networks of networks, though, many of these specializations are possible because of the connections across immigrant groups, specifically because of relations between immigrant entrepreneurial networks and immigrant worker networks.

In a presentation at the American Sociological Association in

1996, Kim Dae Young reported that Korean business owners in New York City were turning away from employing other Koreans because Korean workers were becoming more expensive. Instead, Korean employer networks were linking up with networks of Mexican and Ecuadoran workers, so that Mexicans and Ecuadorans were increasingly occupying the bottom rung of labor in small immigrant Korean businesses.

Light et al. (1999), after pointing out that ethnic networks create opportunities through ethnic economies as well as locate opportunities through ethnic jobs, argued that there was a clear limitation to the view that immigrant networks facilitate entrepreneurship. This limitation was the existence of both heavily entrepreneurial groups and working-class migrations, such as those from Mexico and Central America. Light et al. (1999) therefore expanded the idea of the immigrant economy to include what might be considered multi-ethnic immigrant economies; that is, economies of immigrants in which employers and employees were members of different groups. This type of economy, the authors argued, would come into existence when some immigrant groups are so rich in entrepreneurs that they cannot find co-ethnics to hire and when some groups have so few entrepreneurs that immigrants cannot find jobs in the ethnic economy of their own group.

At this point, one might reflect that although Mexican entrepreneurs in gardening businesses can provide jobs for small numbers of co-ethnics, these small contract activities based on family and friendship networks cannot provide work to all individuals in North America's largest immigrant group. On the other hand, if a Korean business owner needs to employ people outside of the immediate family, the owner is unlikely to find cheap Korean labor. Therefore, ethnic stratification will entail not simply immigrants employed at different levels in the larger economy, but also employing immigrant groups linked to employed immigrant groups.

Light et al. (1999) illustrated this situation with the example of the garment industry in Los Angeles, where immigrants constituted 93 percent of the personnel in 1990. The authors argued that this predominance existed because immigrants had largely created that industry: "The immigrants provided virtually all the financial capital, the human capital, the social capital, the cultural capital, and the labor power that this industry required" (p. 12). Within the industry, Asians were heavily overrepresented among owners and Latinas made up most of the sewers, with few owners of Latin American origin.

Since Light et al. (1999) published their study, the garment industry of Los Angeles has contracted, in part because of competition from Mexico, but also because of regulatory pressures within the United States (Light, 2006). Despite the contraction, though, the industry remains a good illustration of the situation in which there are different immigrant specializations within an immigrant economy. Moreover, it suggests that we can think of social capital as the product of linkages of individuals across categorically defined networks, as well as within networks. Co-ethnic ties apparently enable Koreans to open businesses such as garment shops. The presence of Latino workers, and the channeling of immigrant workers toward garment businesses, though, can also be seen as a kind of social capital that has enabled the owners to be competitive with the global garment industry. The fact that many of these garment factories have been, with some justice, characterized as "sweatshops," with bad working conditions, low wages, and scarce benefits, can be seen as part of the "dark side" of social capital.

The Mixing of Ethnic Economies and Ethnic Jobs

I have distinguished between network channeling of immigrants to ethnic jobs and network interactions that produce what Light et al. (1999) and others have called ethnic economies. Ethnic jobs are mainly group specializations that result from using social ties to find existing opportunities. Ethnic economies are group specializations that result from using social ties to generate new opportunities through entrepreneurship.

As we have seen already, the mixing of ethnic economies and ethnic jobs is common for two reasons. First, some immigrant ethnic economies rely on linkages between members of groups that are specialized in entrepreneurship and members of groups that are specialized in labor. Second, many immigrant groups combine using social ties as means of finding jobs and using social ties as means of creating businesses.

In Chapter 3, I described the Vietnamese as engaging in a mixed adaptation strategy of service jobs, labor, and ethnic economies. Their most common specialization by the twenty-first century was as beauticians and manicurists or pedicurists, and this specialization owed a great deal to ethnic networks, especially kinship networks, as detailed in Chapter 4. Restaurants and small corner shops, typically dependent on the labor of family and friends of family, were other common forms of Vietnamese entrepreneurship, but the Vietnamese had opened a variety of other types of businesses as well. In 2007, Vietnamese Americans owned 229,149 firms, with receipts of $28.8 billion (United States Census Bureau, 2011). Two-thirds of Vietnamese-owned businesses in the United States were in repair, maintenance, personal services, laundry services, and retail sales sectors. The Vietnamese were also employed in a range of occupations. The most common occupations of Vietnamese workers in the United States, according to the 2010 three-year American Community Survey, were, in order of frequency, as assemblers of electrical equipment, unclassified managers and supervisors, supervisors and proprietors of sales jobs, computer systems analysts and computer scientists, cooks, computer software developers, accountants and auditors, cashiers, retail sales clerks, and waiters or waitresses (Ruggles et al., 2010).

The variety of occupations, together with the information on Vietnamese small businesses, might suggest that the Vietnamese were simply spread across ethnic economies, ethnic jobs, and work in the mainstream economy. To some extent this is true, but it is important to recognize how networks based on immigrant group membership link people across seemingly unconnected occupational settings and provide both channeling and collaboration to generate resources. In order to illustrate the interconnections of different strategies, we can turn to the example of Vietnamese employment along the Gulf Coast.

In an earlier study (Bankston and Zhou, 1996), Min Zhou and I found that between 1980 and 1990, fishing and shrimping became a major occupational concentration of Louisiana Vietnamese workers, employing nearly one out of ten individuals in the group. It was also a major source of self-employment. Interestingly, this ethnic economy appears to have begun with the Vietnamese entry into jobs in the mainstream economy that became an ethnic specialization. Like the meat and poultry industries and agriculture, the fishing industry has a demand for low-wage manual labor. Thus, when Indochinese refugees began to arrive in the U.S., "it was considered fortunate that some Gulf Coast seafood companies needed workers to help with fishing and packing, and were receptive to hiring Vietnamese" (Starr, 1981: 227). For example, in August of 1975, the Spence Fishing Company in the Florida Panhandle, motivated by difficulties in finding fishermen, sponsored 300 refugees from Eglin Air Force Base (*Times-Picayune*, 1975). The peripheral sector characteristics of fishing industry labor, namely the low pay and hard physical work, made this a place where newcomers could find jobs.

Some of the Vietnamese had fishing experience in Vietnam, but many did not. As they gained experience of the industry, though, they were able to turn what had been ethnic jobs into an ethnic economy by turning interpersonal relations into assets. The interpersonal relations aided them in the two ways in which ethnic social capital usually enables entrepreneurship: raising funds and providing labor. In our study, Min Zhou and I quoted Monsignor Dominic Luong, pastor of Louisiana's largest Vietnamese Catholic church and one of the leading spokesmen of Vietnamese Americans:

> Some Americans were asking me, "how is it that you people just come to America and almost right away you can buy houses and have all these things?" So I took them out to visit some families to see how we live and how we manage to come up with the money to buy our homes. Two families will move in together and all work and save their money. Or someone who doesn't have a home will move in with a relative who owns one and won't have to pay any rent, so they can save all their money until they can buy a home of their own. (Luong,

personal communication, March 15, 1993, quoted in Bankston and Zhou, 1996: 48)

As we observe in the study, strategies that enable people to buy houses also enable them to buy boats. Further, we found that virtually all Vietnamese captains had exclusively Vietnamese crews, who worked for shares of the catch, so that labor costs were low. Further still, this contributed to the growth of other ethnic economic activities. During the 1980s, Hai Minh Huynh, owner of Fulton Seafood in Venice, Louisiana, became one of the state's largest seafood buyers (Ashton, 1985). Nguyen Cao Ky, former premier of South Vietnam, became owner and manager of a shrimp processing plant in Dulac, Louisiana. Ky explicitly mentioned the growing predominance of Vietnamese around the area of Dulac in shrimping, and his ties to them, as the reason he was able to establish this business (Schlifstein, 1988) Our interviews with Louisiana Vietnamese restaurant owners suggested that they purchased most of their seafood from Vietnamese fishermen (Bankston and Zhou, 1996).

Once activities in the seafood industry had been established as an ethnic specialization for the Vietnamese, network linkages led them to branch out geographically and occupationally. During the 1980s, Richard Gollot, owner of the Golden Gulf Seafood processing factory in Biloxi, Mississippi, in an effort to obtain low-cost labor, reportedly began recruiting Vietnamese from the Louisiana seafood industry, establishing a critical bridging tie. Once other Vietnamese heard from co-ethnics that there were jobs available in Mississippi, they began moving and getting jobs through their interpersonal connections (Bankston, 2012b).

The growing Vietnamese population often sought housing in East Biloxi in order to be near the coast and the processing plants. Small Vietnamese-owned businesses grew up around East Biloxi and then in other nearby locations, at first in order to sell foods and services to the ethnic community, but later to invest the money earned in processing plants in shops, including manicure and beauty shops, serving other groups.

In 1991, Biloxi decided to allow gambling, and this rapidly

became a growth industry. When a few Vietnamese found jobs in casino gambling, they brought in co-ethnics, and by the year 2000 casino gambling was becoming an ethnic niche industry for local Vietnamese. Estimates from the 2000 Census showed that over 18 percent of employed Vietnamese people in Mississippi worked in eating and drinking places, representing a heavy concentration in restaurants. Another 13 percent worked in fisheries, although this was a proportional decline from 1990 (before gambling), when 18 percent were in fisheries. Another 10 percent in 2000 worked in entertainment and recreation industries, which reflected work in gambling (Bankston, 2012b).

The point of this example is to illustrate how seemingly disparate occupational niches actually result from movement along network lines and from network collaboration within niches. The Vietnamese began with ethnic jobs in fishing and fisheries, developed ethnic economies on the basis of these, and established self-employment, employment with co-ethnics, employment serving co-ethnics, and employment in the mainstream economy through patterns of interactions that branched out in the style of fractal geometry.

There is some similarity in the Vietnamese example to the Mexican example described in the section on ethnic jobs. In both, there are general specializations, but also a mixing of workforce strategies, including small-scale ethnic entrepreneurship, working for co-ethnics, and employment in mainstream industries that hire immigrant workers. In both, different types of economic activity depend on different types of networks. Vietnamese restaurants or small shops rely heavily on kin and other close ties, as do Mexican lawn care businesses. Finding work in a seafood processing factory in Mississippi or in a poultry processing plant in Georgia depends on information spread through wider ethnic networks. In both, the mixing of ethnic economies and ethnic jobs tends to take place within a limited socioeconomic range, mostly at the bottom of the stratification system. However, we should also note that there are differences. Buying fishing boats requires more capital than buying lawnmowers. The community network differences between Vietnamese and Mexican immigrants generally make more potentially profitable forms of ethnic entrepreneurship available to the former. Even though immigrants of both groups specialize in jobs that are often considered hard and dirty, the more collaborative interpersonal networks of the newly arrived refugee-origin group tend to be better able to turn social capital into financial capital, at least for some immigrants.

Ethnic Professions

In a summary overview of immigration published in 1994, prominent immigration research Rubén G. Rumbaut observed that immigrants to the United States since World War II could be classified according to socioeconomic status as professionals, entrepreneurs, and manual laborers. In the present chapter, I have looked at the entrepreneurial immigrants as creators of ethnic economies and at the manual laborers as members of a new, largely Spanish-speaking working class. I have then suggested that in practice many immigrant ethnic groups combine entrepreneurial and laboring specializations.

Both the entrepreneurs and the workers rely, in different ways, on interpersonal networks; the former primarily to generate opportunities through collaboration and low-cost labor, and the latter chiefly to find opportunities through information along network lines. For the professional immigrants, though, the economic role of ethnic networks is less clear. Immigrants who find work as engineers, physicians, nurses, or professors obtain their jobs through mainstream businesses. Immigrating as professionals, they are often recruited by these businesses even before entering the country. The most obvious transnational networks behind their movement are institutional networks, such as educational institutions and recruiting agencies in the homeland with ties to American companies, rather than the kinds of interpersonal networks that enable immigrant entrepreneurs to start businesses and immigrant laborers to find jobs (Acacio, 2007).

Despite the apparent importance of formal mechanisms for placing professional immigrants in jobs, though, informal interpersonal networks channel professionals, as well as laborers, into occupational niches. Roger Waldinger, studying immigrants in professional occupations in New York City, argued that professional niche concentrations of immigrants grew through informal network mechanisms, as well as formal recruiting of professionals into places unfilled by natives. After positions in the city bureaucracy opened up to immigrants and some individuals found places, network recruiting of kin, friends, and other co-ethnics brought immigrants into professional jobs, operating transnationally as well as locally. Waldinger quotes an executive in an engineering agency:

> There seems to be a tremendous network of friends and family; real contacts socially. Even in the past when we were first conducting our own provisional hiring pools, with no lists, we would post or gather resumes, send out call letters, and then have them come to hiring pools. We would invite 50 people and 80 would show up, "Oh, my brother's friend's cousin called and said there would be a position." Once we had a recruitment for managers and engineers by invitation only. And there was somebody who flew in from India that day. (Waldinger, 1994: 22)

Waldinger found that as immigrants became insiders, they became privy to vacancies and they passed news about these vacancies on to their family and community members. Human capital did come into play, as in other immigrant professional niches. Waldinger noted that immigrants who concentrated in the bureaucracy were good test-takers, and therefore able to do well on civil service tests. But selective information channels brought them to the tests. Again, a "dark side" of social capital appears, since the exclusionary bias (or "opportunity hoarding") of network recruitment caused resentment on the part of native minorities.

Immigrant professional networks are not unique to government employment. As I have pointed out in Chapter 3, in the examination of Filipinos as professional immigrants to an aging America, nursing is a clear professional occupational niche among Filipino immigrants to the United States, and nurses of Filipino origin have become the single largest ethnic group within this profession. A survey conducted by the Commission on Graduates of Foreign Nursing Schools in 2001 found that 41 percent of respondents had obtained nursing degrees in the Philippines (Berger, 2003). The contextual setting for this professional specialization was created by the training of healthcare professionals in the Philippines by American colonial officials, exchange programs for Filipino nurses during the 1950s and 1960s, and demand for nurses in the United States influencing U.S. immigration policy (Choy, 2003). Within this context, though, social networks have contributed to maintaining this immigrant professional niche. As more nurses arrived in the United States during the 1960s, they observed the sharp contrast between the medical facilities available in America and those available back in the Philippines. Further, these professional immigrants experienced a high level of consumption. These immigrant nurses communicated the advantages of working in the United States to friends and family back in the Philippines, helping to create what Catherine Ceniza Choy (2003) has called a "culture of migration," with nursing widely perceived among Filipino social circles as desirable precisely because it gave opportunities for migration. Information networks were shaping the acquisition of human capital for purposes of international resettlement.

Within the United States, the "cumulative causation" of increasing representation of Filipinos, and especially of Filipinas, within nursing has led to an ethnic identification with the profession. At Montefiore Medical Center in New York City, pediatric instructor Clemencia S. Wong observed that "if you meet a Filipino girl [*sic*] and say, 'you're a nurse,' you're probably right" (Berger, 2003: B1). Even among women of Filipino origin born or growing up in the United States, the fact that so many social contacts are nurses acts as a strong encouragement to incline toward this professional specialization. Working in hospitals and clinics, Filipino nurses also find out about vacancies. Although they may not have as much ability as Waldinger's government bureaucrats to limit information to their own group members, they are insiders who can help place their friends. In my own informal interviews with Filipino immigrants in the United States, I have found repeatedly that social gatherings of co-ethnics are precisely where information about job openings, in medical establishments and elsewhere, is transmitted.

Historically produced human capital and labor market demand, then, only establish the broader settings for accounting for the specialization of immigrant groups within professions. Relatively advantageous socioeconomic concentrations of immigrant groups occur within these settings through a kind of insider trading in social capital. Professional immigrant networks, then, can be seen as one way in which immigrant groups differentially promote the socioeconomic adaptation of their own group members.

8

Adaptation: Educational Attainment
and Achievement

Educational performance has long been one of the primary areas of social capital research. James S. Coleman, the influential sociological theorist of social capital, argued that structures of social relations can account for differences in educational performance across families and across communities. He maintained that parental interest in children's learning can promote academic achievement even when the parents have little human capital. Moreover, social capital in a community allows parents "to establish norms and reinforce each other's sanctioning of the children" (Coleman, 1990: 318). From this perspective, social capital within the family and the community, inherent in the social structures of some ethnic groups, can help generate human capital in the second generation (Coleman, 1988).

Following Coleman, educational versions of social capital theory have tended to emphasize the importance of dense, transitive ties within communities. While researchers have debated when and whether weak ties can promote occupational upward mobility for individuals and groups by bringing in useful information, social capital accounts of success in education have generally focused on the control and direction provided by bonding ties in immigrant families and communities. Insofar as researchers have considered bridging ties to outsiders as an influence on the school performance of children in immigrant groups, they have looked mainly at connections between immigrants and school personnel (see, for example, Stanton-Salazar and Dornbusch, 1995).

The idea that social capital for educational advancement may consist of linkages between interpersonal networks and formal institutions is consistent with the arguments of Robert Putnam (1995; 2000), who portrayed membership in organizations such as parent–teacher organizations and associations (PTOs and PTAs) as vital sources of generalized social capital. However, while there may be differences in the degree of involvement of parents from different immigrant groups in the schooling of their children, if parents' connections to schools constitute the most important social asset for immigrant children, then immigrant networks per se would tend to be liabilities because immigrant families generally have fewer connections to schools (Kao and Rutherford, 2007). As Patricia Fernández Kelly (2002: 81) has perceptively observed, "ethnic institutions almost by definition do not provide a large number of external links. Their role is to maximize internal resources and to supply the needs of groups that have either recently arrived . . . or been left behind by the hardening of ethnic demarcations." Network closure entails an inward concentration of social ties, limiting linkages to institutions and people outside the ethnic group. In what situations, then, would immigrant network closure contribute to educational achievement and attainment?

Min Zhou and I (Zhou and Bankston, 1998) argued that members of immigrant groups often settle in relatively low-income areas, in which young people frequently have little expectation of educational success and upward mobility. In this setting, immigrant social networks can provide alternatives to assimilation into disadvantaged segments of contemporary society and encourage mobility through education. This segmented assimilation version of social capital theory assumes that networks within immigrant communities can direct young people toward educational achievement and attainment, and the assumption implies that the content of information in a network is important. Even if adult immigrants have little knowledge of the educational system of the host society, they must place a high value on education, or network constraints and supports will not encourage school success.

In addition, the fact that immigrant networks can provide alternatives to disadvantaged settings does not mean that these networks can only promote success for immigrants in low-income neighborhoods with limited human capital. The segmented assimilation approach to social capital is compensatory. Those who lack not only financial resources but immediate social resources in their places of settlement can turn inward to their own ethnic networks. Again, this assumes that supports, controls, and drive toward the future exist inside their enclaves. Here, the distinction just quoted, made by Fernández Kelly (2002), may be important for understanding why supports, controls, and drive may be greater inside some immigrant networks than others. The recently arrived groups can exist largely separate from their immediate surroundings. Groups with well-established positions in American society, such as Mexicans, face well-established barriers and socioeconomic channels in the larger society, and those barriers and channels have often been internalized into the expectations of ethnic networks.

Immigrant social ties may be complementary, though, as well as compensatory. The children of an immigrant physician, for example, may well live in a fairly affluent neighborhood surrounded by peers and adults with high expectations. Still, even these children of immigrants may receive extra social investments from co-ethnic associates if their associates share their own families' drive to achievement. Social networks do not only connect families and communities to schools or generate assets (or liabilities) that students bring to schools. Social networks also exist within schools and these may sometimes have greater immediate influence than family and community networks outside of school. Kimberly A. Goyette and Gilberto Q. Conchas (2002) compared sets of Vietnamese American and Mexican American students and found that the former studied more because they had more positive peer associations and more supportive relationships with teachers than the latter. Along somewhat similar lines, Stanton-Salazar (2001) found that the school adaptation of low-income Mexican-origin students depended on how peer networks and support systems in schools fit together with family and community in the larger context of American society.

If relationships with peers and teachers affect school performance, though, we need to ask what shapes those in-school relationships. In my previous research, I have found that social capital in the school is derived from families and communities. Students bring expectations and experiences to school from their families and neighborhoods and invest these in each other in school, and students invest the habits and characteristics that they bring from outside the school in relationships with their teachers.

The matter of shared expectations raises the question of whether immigrant human capital derived from country of origin social structures influences the capacity of networks to convey useful information (see Figure 3.1). Cynthia Feliciano (2006) found that one of the reasons the children of relatively advantaged immigrant groups tend to do well in school is that the pre-migration educational status of an immigrant group and the group's average post-migration socioeconomic status were related to higher perceived educational aspirations among parents and to higher educational expectations among students. It is important to note that Feliciano found this group-level socioeconomic status operating beyond the level of the family. I believe this suggests we need to broaden the limited scope of segmented assimilation approaches to the education of immigrant children by recognizing that immigrant networks can be not only a means of overcoming disadvantages but also a means of passing on pre-migration socioeconomic advantages through family and community networks.

Family and community networks, whether compensatory or complementary, influence students directly by constraining and directing attitudes and behavior relevant to school performance. These networks also influence students indirectly, though, by contributing to what Suárez-Orozco and Suárez-Orozco (2007) have called "relational engagement," "meaningful and supportive relationships in school, with adults as well as peers" (p. 251). Considering relational engagement, or within-school social capital, in addition to family and community relationships can help us understand why there are educational differences across groups and to conceptualize how interpersonal networks maintain and reproduce ethnic stratification.

Network Constraints on Education

The existence of group differences in educational outcomes related to immigration is clear. Figures 8.1 and 8.2 illustrate variations in two of these outcomes: high school completion and college completion, taken from Census data presented by the National Center for Education Statistics (NCES) (United States Department of Education, 2010). Figure 8.1 shows status dropout rates among selected groups of native-born and foreign-born young people. Status dropout rates are percentages of 16– to 24–year-olds who are neither enrolled in school nor high school graduates. Here, the race and Hispanic ethnicity categories are not mutually exclusive, so whites, blacks, and (to a very small degree) Asians do include Hispanics, especially among the foreign-born.

One should keep in mind in looking at this figure that Hispanics

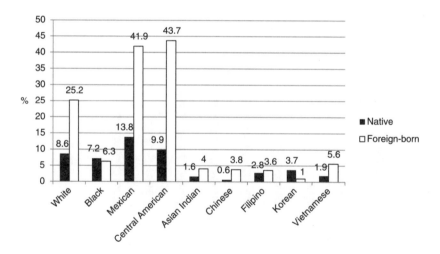

Figure 8.1 Native and Foreign-Born Status Dropout Rates (Aged 16–24 and Not in School or Graduate) for Selected Native-Born and Foreign-Born Groups, 2005

Note: Race and ethnicity are not mutually exclusive in this figure.

Source: United States Department of Education, 2007: table 17b.

and Asians make up about three-quarters of immigrants to the United States, and that heavy immigration from Latin America and Asia since 1980 means that many of the native-born young people in these regional classifications are children of immigrants. Native-born Mexicans and Central Americans had higher dropout rates than native-born whites and blacks. All of the native-born Asian national-origin categories, on the other hand, had substantially lower dropout rates than native-born whites or blacks. Asian immigrants of all categories except Koreans showed higher dropout rates than Asians born in the United States, but even Asian immigrants had lower dropout rates than white, black, Mexican, or Central American natives. Overall, the most striking difference is between members of the two regional categories that contain most of the immigrants and children of immigrants: high dropout rates among Mexicans and Central Americans, low dropout rates among Asians.

Figure 8.2 shows the same kinds of variations in college

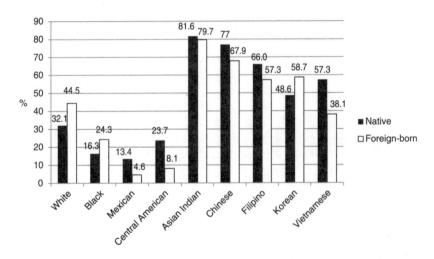

Figure 8.2 Native- and Foreign-Born Percentages of Individuals Aged 25–9 with at Least a Bachelor's Degree, for Selected Native-Born and Foreign-Born Groups, 2007

Source: United States Department of Education, 2010: table 27b.

completion among young adults. While native-born Central Americans showed higher college completion rates than native-born blacks, in general those in the Hispanic categories showed the lowest college completion rates and those in the Asian categories showed the highest completion rates. It is notable that Mexicans born in the United States were less likely to have finished a bachelor's degree than immigrants in any of the groups.

Why do these differences exist? One structural answer to this question has to do with the selectivity of the labor market for immigrants. If, as noted earlier, people cross the Mexican–U.S. border to take jobs within the new Spanish-speaking working class, then many Mexicans will have relatively low levels of education because they arrive to take jobs that do not require substantial formal schooling. This is undoubtedly part of the reason that so many Mexican-origin young people have limited credentials, but it cannot completely account for the phenomenon, because Mexican-origin youth born in the United States were more likely to have dropped out of school than any of the native-born or foreign-born in any other racial or ethnic category except foreign-born whites (a category that includes Mexicans and other Hispanics). Similarly, native-born Mexicans in the 25–9 age category were less likely to have completed college than any other native-born or foreign-born category except for foreign-born Mexicans and Central Americans.

A similar labor market recruitment explanation might account for part of the extremely high levels of college completion among Asians. Many Asian Indian, Chinese, and Filipino immigrants do enter the United States as professional immigrants and will therefore arrive with degrees in hand. While this would not account for the fact that in most of the Asian categories the native-born are even more likely to have completed college than immigrants, this last fact could be attributed to transmission of human capital: highly educated parents tend to rear children who can also attain credentials. The problem with taking labor markets and transmission of human capital as the entire explanation, though, is that the Asian groups vary substantially in both professional employment and immigrant-generation human capital. As Min Zhou and I noted in our book on Vietnamese American children (1998) and in many other publications, the Vietnamese entered as members of a refugee group without a pre-established socioeconomic location and with generally very limited human capital. Yet, as Figures 8.1 and 8.2 show, Vietnamese young people have demonstrated high educational attainment, compared to Americans in general and to immigrants from Latin America.

The transmission of human capital explanation, moreover, raises questions about how parents transmit human capital. Is it only a matter of resources (such as books in the home) or does it also involve parent–child relationships? If it is a matter of relationships, is it limited to ties within families or do these relationships also include ties with neighbors and peers?

On the labor market recruitment explanation of high Mexican dropout rates, Rogelio Saenz and Carlos Siordia (2012) have found that dropout rates among Mexican-origin young people could be primarily attributed to inter-cohort reproduction. Saenz and Siordia look at Mexican dropout rates across cohorts in geographical regions defined by the Census, finding relatively high dropout rates among members of a younger cohort who live in a Public Use Microdata Area (PUMA) with members of an older cohort with high dropout rates.

To account for this transmission of low educational attainment across age cohorts, one can begin with the setting of Mexican American communities. The movement of Mexicans to new destinations in the U.S. has not decreased their residential isolation. In fact, the growth and dispersion of the Mexican population have been accompanied by the intensifying segregation of Mexican-origin communities (Lichter, 2010). Both the communities in which those in the new Spanish-speaking working class live and the schools that their children attend are highly segregated. Suárez-Orozco and Suárez-Orozco (2007: 249) have remarked that "Latino youth are now the most segregated students in American schools." In 2010, over 60 percent of Hispanic students in the United States attended schools in counties in which minorities made up majorities of the public school populations (Bankston, 2012c).

Both the community and in-school interpersonal networks of Latino young people, most of whom are of Mexican origin, are highly isolated, with relatively few bridging ties. Understanding how this isolation tends to constrain rather than enable academic achievement and attainment requires that one consider the information available in the networks of these young people and the organization of linkages within those networks. The information available to young people comes from the experiences of their interpersonal connections. Suárez-Orozco (1987) and Matute-Bianchi (1986; 1991) have described the outlooks of Mexican American teenagers as consequences of generations of discrimination and isolation. In contrast to members of more recently arrived groups, the information about chances for life improvement that moves through their network lines is about barriers to opportunity, not paths to opportunity. In his overview of the nature of social capital, Alejandro Portes (1998) describes this situation as a form of negative social capital, in which downward-leveling social norms direct young people away from school performance rather than toward it.

Compounding the problem of shared norms and expectations derived from information about historical experiences, contemporary adult experiences provide limited and highly specific information about life in the United States. The members of the new Spanish-speaking working class can mainly communicate about their own positions. On this point, Saenz and Cready (2004) found that social ties enabled new immigrants to find jobs, but that community social capital, in the form of links to co-ethnics, was negatively associated with upward mobility. Similarly, co-ethnic social connections for younger members of the group are ties with people who have limited human capital and few linkages outside of a constricted socioeconomic range.

This constraining effect of social ties to others who can generally bring little information relevant to upward mobility through schooling operates at the level of communities, peer groups, and families. Consequently, the influence of ties varies according to the information these network levels can bring to young people. In looking at the relationship between social capital and familism,

Valenzuela and Dornbusch (1994) found a positive association between strong family attachments and academic achievement for Mexican American students only for those whose parents had completed at least 12 years of school. One can interpret this as indicating that family relations contribute to school performance only when parents in this group can communicate on the basis of sufficient human capital.

Ream and Rumberger (2008) attributed high dropout rates among Mexican Americans in part to the influence of peer group networks. These authors argued that students who are highly engaged in school tend to have friends who are also highly engaged in school. Members of school-oriented friendship networks reinforce and intensify dedication to schooling, while disengaged networks encourage alienation from formal education. Ream and Rumberger find that Mexican-origin students are less engaged than whites in organized academic activities and formally sponsored extracurricular activities, and that the disengagement is encouraged by their friends. Note, here, that peer group connections within schools are often to other minority students in a setting of disadvantage, and not to adults who arrived in the United States seeking opportunity and who may be able to communicate some version of this mobility orientation to young people.

The highly segregated setting of Mexican-origin students means that the schools they attend concentrate students with comparatively little attachment to schooling, so that the peer contacts within those schools are among young people who share and foster academic disengagement. There is relatively little peer social capital in the form of friendships that pay off in schooling. Students coming from families and communities that concentrate low human capital in isolated settings bring their experiences and expectations to their associations with peers, so that peer networks intensify constraints.

Previous chapters noted that the contemporary Spanish-speaking working class is highly mobile geographically and directed toward manual labor and low-paid industrial occupations. Labor market specialization tends to channel young people, as well as adults. At the same time, geographic mobility and competition for jobs undermine solidarity and cohesion, so that network organization is generally not conducive to mobilizing for intergenerational upward mobility through the schools.

Before moving on to looking at ways in which social capital can produce positive outcomes, I want to note that one should avoid falling into network fatalism. Although Latino high school dropout rates are still much higher than those of other racial and ethnic groups in the United States, they have been going down in the early twenty-first century (Fry and Taylor, 2012). Further, while cross-sectional studies generally show poor outcomes in educational attainment among Mexican Americans, cohort and longitudinal studies have shown substantial rates of mobility (Smith, 2003; 2006). The reasons for the apparent educational advances among Latino young people are unclear, but the trends do indicate that one should not take network constraints on mobility as either unchanging or deterministic.

Social Capital to Financial Capital to Human Capital

Figures 8.1 and 8.2 show that all of the Asian-origin groups have substantially lower high school dropout rates and substantially higher college attendance rates than native-born or immigrant whites, blacks, Mexicans, or Central Americans. The high average level of academic achievement among groups that arrive to meet the contemporary demand for professionals with high human capital may not be surprising. One would expect the children of doctors, nurses, and educators to pursue schooling, although even among these groups ethnic social networks can help to explain how human capital is transmitted across generations (as will be seen in the next section). However, all of the Asian groups show high school attainment. To explain this, we can reflect that the Asian groups in general have come from much more distant locations than Mexico or Central America and do not constitute a continuing supply of low-cost labor for the United States.

In addition, many of the Asian arrivals are entrepreneurial immigrants, with strong mobility orientations and networks that maintain and intensify those orientations. Immigrant entrepreneurs make use of family and co-ethnic social networks in order to establish and maintain their businesses. However, entrepreneurs often do not aim at achieving a measure of financial success as an end in itself. Instead, they intend to use their businesses in order to create a basis for upward mobility for their children.

Intergenerational mobility among entrepreneurial immigrant groups through investment in education has a long history. Steinberg (1981; 1986) studied Jewish immigrant entrepreneurs in the late nineteenth- to early twentieth-century wave of immigration and found that owners of small businesses used profits to invest in the educations of their children, leading to professionalization of the American-born generation. Similarly, Bonacich and Modell (1980) found that entrepreneurship among Japanese immigrants resulted in increased educational attainment for their children, and others have found historical associations between immigrant entrepreneurship and younger generation educational mobility among both Japanese and Chinese immigrants (see, for example, Hirschman and Wong, 1986; Nee and Wong, 1985; Sanchirico, 1991).

Clearly, if family and community supports enable immigrants to establish businesses and businesses enable investment in schooling, social capital can be transformed into human capital through building financial capital. However, the network linkages behind ethnic entrepreneurship can also advance educational attainment more directly. Because parents put long, hard hours into small business activities specifically for the purpose of encouraging mobility through education among their children, the work of the parents becomes part of communicating the mobility orientation to the children. Further, the same co-ethnic links that contribute to entrepreneurship in the parental generation reinforce the direction and channeling of children toward professionalization.

Kim (1993: 231) has observed the transformation of the mobility orientation across generations among heavily entrepreneurial Korean immigrants:

The cultural model of success held by Korean immigrants dictates different strategies for different types of people within the group depending on age at the time of immigration: Whereas immigrants should make it through "hard work" in "their own businesses," children of immigrants who were born in the United States or came to the United States at a young age and therefore do not have language or cultural barriers should "study hard," "go to the most prestigious schools," and "become professionals."

Kim (1993) notes that the model of first-generation financial success through entrepreneurship and second-generation professional success through education permeates Korean American thought at the level of the community as well as at that of the family: "this immigrant type of cultural model mobilizes the whole community to exert community forces and thereby directs and controls community members' lives" (p. 233). It is not just that parents in small businesses communicate the message of mobility through education to their children. Members of the parent generation transmit this message to each other and reinforce each family's emphasis on the pursuit of degrees in professional fields, especially from elite selective institutions. "The zeal for their children's education possessed by Korean immigrants and their community is summarized by one student's statement that 'the whole Korean community worships Harvard'" (Kim, 1993: 233).

The long hours that entrepreneurial parents put into their businesses and the pressures they place on their children can create generation gaps. Just as pressure for conformity can have the unintended consequence of ostracizing some young people, the intense pressure for school success can, in some cases, result in psychological stress and rebellion. Koreans, in Figures 8.1 and 8.2, are the only Asians who show higher high school dropout rates and lower college completion rates among the native-born than among the foreign-born. On this point, I will note that the education statistics for Koreans that the NCES gives are at odds with the findings of Sakamoto and Xie (2006), using 2000 data, that 46 percent of foreign-born Koreans and 61 percent of native-born had completed college. Despite this apparent anomaly in the NCES data, though, Figures 8.1 and 8.2 are consistent with the argument that the entrepreneurial mobility orientation of adult immigrants tends to translate into an educational mobility orientation for children.

The social capital–financial capital–human capital trajectory of upward mobility is a way in which immigrants at the margins of the socioeconomic system can mobilize social resources to move children into relatively advantageous positions in the mainstream of the American economy. Another look at Figure 8.2, though, shows that the national-origin groups with the highest rates of college completion among young adults are, in order, Asian Indians, Chinese, and Filipinos. Both the native-born and foreign-born young people of all of these groups are far more likely to complete higher education than are native-born whites. While all three of these groups do contain entrepreneurs (such as the Gujarati motel owners discussed in Chapter 7), these three groups are notable for the heavy representation of professional immigrants.

If the social linkages associated with entrepreneurial activities can be a source of educational advancement among immigrant children and children of immigrants, coming from an entrepreneurial family background is not the only path forward through the educational system. Dae Young Kim (2006) found that Korean children of entrepreneurial immigrants and Korean children of professional immigrants both generally fare well educationally and occupationally, compared to others in the United States, but that the children of professionals show some advantages over the children of entrepreneurs. Of course, the children of immigrant professionals enjoy human capital advantages within their own families. Parents with professional jobs in the United States not only have economic resources to invest in the schooling of their children, they also have knowledge about educational systems directly relevant to the American academic environment. Among professional immigrants, though, co-ethnic ties can provide complementary social capital.

Professional and Subtle Networks and Social Capital

Zhou (1997: 66) notes that "[w]hile many immigrants continue to follow the traditional bottom-up route, significant numbers of new arrivals have bypassed the bottom starting line and moved directly into mainstream labor markets while dispersing into suburban middle-class communities." This pathway directly into the middle class (or upper middle class) for some immigrant groups is a consequence of the vast socioeconomic diversity of contemporary immigrant groups (Zhou, 1997).

On this point, Feliciano's (2006) finding that the pre-migration educational status of a group is related to higher expectations among adults and students has clear implications for the role of social circles among students with immigrant parents in professional occupations. If group educational background leads to high expectations, then these expectations, logically, result from association with group members. Not only do parents communicate their goals to their own children, but they also communicate those same goals to the children of co-ethnic friends. Young people who associate with other young people from the same background continually find these goals reinforced among their peers.

Moreover, immigrant social circles contribute to school performance even beyond socioeconomic background because the immigrant mobility orientation spurs on professionals, as well as entrepreneurs. Harris, Jamison, and Trujillo (2008), examining nationally representative data, found that "the academic disadvantage observed among Mexican and Puerto Rican immigrants [*sic*] relative to whites is largely explained by their lower SES [socioeconomic status]" (p. 110). Among Asian immigrants, though, "academic advantages ... relative to whites are partially explained by their socioeconomic characteristics and fully explained by their immigrant and socioeconomic characteristics combined" (p. 110).

One of the explanations of Asian immigrant academic achievement that has received substantial support in the literature is the "relative functionalism" account offered by Sue and Okazaki (1990). In this view, the occupational opportunities of Asians, especially immigrant Asians, can be found mainly through formal education because they have limited informal connections that would provide other avenues. Thus, their mobility orientations focus on education. While this explanation is relevant to Asian immigrants in general, it is especially relevant to professional immigrants because those in the parent generation owe many of their own opportunities to human capital even when they are able to use in-group social ties to create professional niches for group members.

Part of the generally high level of educational attainment and achievement among children of professional Chinese and Asian Indian immigrants, then, can be attributed to the fact that group members identify advanced education as an ethnic niche. Strategies such as weekend schools enable the professional immigrants to direct their children toward this niche (Zhou, 1997). At the same time, informal connections with other group members and formal ethnic organizations, such as those described by Brettell (2005) among Asian Indians in Dallas–Fort Worth, channel the children of professional immigrants toward concentration on schooling.

One can easily see how highly visible professional immigrant groups that manage accommodation without assimilation can maintain ethnic networks that direct young people in the accumulation of human capital. But what about less visible and more subtle immigrant networks? As I detailed in Chapters 5 and 6, using the example of Filipinos, outwardly "assimilated" immigrant groups that operate in many ways in the mainstream of the society, as well as the economy, often employ ethnic network connections to provide children with complementary social capital.

Although students of Filipino origin on average have higher levels of academic achievement than white American students, the achievement of the former is generally lower than that of Asian Indians or Chinese. Comparing Filipino and Chinese national origin adolescents, Eng et al. (2008) found that the Filipinos had weaker scholastic performance. Eng et al. also found, though, that

Filipino students who were more acculturated in American society tended to perform worse than those who were less acculturated, a finding that indicates the relevance of ethnic connections for the academic achievement of Filipinos.

In an article devoted primarily to what can be considered the dark side of social capital, Diane Wolf provides some insight into how ethnic connections at the family level are associated with Filipino academic achievement. Wolf (1997: 457) notes that "in general, post-1965 Filipino immigrants have been predominantly middle-class, college-educated, English-speaking professionals who integrate easily into the labor force and quickly blend into the American landscape." Despite the outward assimilation, though, the young Filipino immigrants and children of immigrants Wolf interviewed identified highly distinctive ethnic ties, especially kinship ties, as influences on their lives. For example, when Wolf asked her respondents, "what does it mean to you to be a Filipino?" one representative response was:

I guess the get-togethers are the big thing because family is just so important. The structure of the family is important with being Filipino because I know families who don't really talk outside the first cousins but my family has always kept in touch with 8th and 9th cousins. We all know each other and we speak to them all the time because we call them and stuff even though it's not a holiday. (Wolf, 1997: 462)

Within these family networks, Wolf observes, one of the main messages communicated to children is the importance of education:

In response to our question as to whether Vallejo teachers and high school counselors noticed anything particular about their Filipino students as compared with their nonFilipino students, particularly the children of immigrants, most responded without hesitation, referring to the intense academic pressure Filipino students of immigrants, especially Filipinas, receive from parents. This pressure was attributed to parents being immigrants, their desire to succeed, and their desire for their children to achieve at least their same middle to upper middle class status. (Wolf, 1997: 463)

173

Living largely outside of enclaves, young people of Filipino ancestry are usually not surrounded by webs of transitive relations within co-ethnic networks to the extent that many other children of immigrants are, especially if the former have only one parent of Filipino ancestry. Nevertheless, frequent contacts with parents' Filipino friends and associates in the informal gatherings and formal associations discussed in Chapters 5 and 6 can provide networks that reinforce the educational emphases of parents and extended family members. In my own observations of people of Filipino origin with spouses who are not Filipino, I have noted that graduation parties and celebrations of academic achievement are major events even among these maritally assimilated immigrants.

Although immigrants from the Philippines do maintain ethnic networks and these do appear to encourage school performance, it is also the case that the identification of Filipino American children with their parents' ethnic groups is often weaker than the identification of some children in some other groups with the ethnic groups of their parents. As noted, students of Filipino origin show strong academic performance relative to the majority American population, but somewhat weaker performance compared to children of Asian Indian and Chinese background. Moreover, more acculturated children of many immigrant groups, including Filipinos, often do less well in school than less acculturated children. It would be overly speculative and simplistic to attribute all ethnic educational stratification to the extent to which children in different groups are bound up in their own ethnic networks. Among other complications, positions in the socioeconomic system affect the types of information available in networks. Still, it does appear that immigrant network supports and constraints play an important part in the abilities of economically marginal immigrants to generate compensatory social capital for schooling and in the abilities of economically advantaged immigrants to generate complementary social capital.

What happens, though, when networks are unable to support and direct some children? Growing up in the United States is frequently a source of tension between immigrant parents and their children, and children of immigrant groups often resist their parents' and communities' efforts and social control. In addition, interpersonal ties based on immigrant ethnicity can weaken across time and generations. To address the implications for educational mobility of these kinds of developments, the final section in this chapter turns to the issue of weakening networks and possible generational decline.

Weakening Networks and Generational Decline

The phrase "second-generation decline" is usually associated with a controversial argument made by Herbert J. Gans (1992). Gans maintained that we could not assume upward mobility for the children of post-1965 immigrants. He suggested that the children of poor immigrants, especially the darker-skinned children, might not be able to find jobs in the mainstream economy and they might be unable or unwilling to take the low-wage, long-hour marginal jobs of their parents. As a result, the descendants of many poorer immigrants could join many low-income African Americans and native-born Hispanics permanently outside the mainstream economy.

The Gans argument was one of the sources of the "segmented assimilation" view; that is, the argument that children of immigrants faced multiple paths, including entry into the middle class for children of professional immigrants, assimilation into the most deprived segment of American society for the poorer immigrant children who assimilated directly into their immediate social settings, and mobility through education for those who bypassed disadvantaged settings through involvement in immigrant social circles. The generational decline argument, as presented by Gans, and its segmented assimilation implications have not been universally accepted. In one particularly useful response, Roger Waldinger and Cynthia Feliciano (2004) have questioned what they see as the pessimism in this line of thinking. Comparing the job-holding rates of first- and second-generation Mexicans with those of African Americans, Puerto Ricans, and native whites, Waldinger and Feliciano have found no support for the claim that the offspring of working-class immigrants will experience downward assimilation.

Seeing the alternatives for less advantaged immigrants as either assimilation into some version of an underclass or upward mobility through the social resources of ethnic separatism may indeed be simplistic. As I have argued throughout this book, the assets that ethnic networks can provide to their members do not depend solely on their closure or even on their internal structures of centrality, transitivity, and hierarchy, but also on the position of the immigrant groups in American society and economy. That position shapes internal network structures, the ways in which the networks link to outsiders, and the kinds of information that flow along lines of social ties. The pay-off of being embedded in an ethnic network depends on which network is being considered. In addition, Waldinger and Feliciano are correct that there are more options in the American economy for children of immigrants than just movement into the professional middle class or dropping out of the labor force altogether. Even though the United States no longer has the factory economy of the early twentieth century, and working-class opportunities are much more limited today than in the past, the most pessimistic scenario for children of the working class is only one of many paths these children may take.

While generational mobility may be more complicated than simply moving upward through networks or downward through immediate assimilation, though, there is clear evidence that immigrant group involvement is related to educational success and that the movement of individuals away from immigrant networks is associated with some forms of generational decline. Succeeding generations of immigrants may not all become part of an underclass permanently outside the labor force, but they do appear to lose ground relative to first-generation children, if those children have both sufficient command of English and extensive ties to their own immigrant backgrounds.

The high dropout rates and low college completion rates among foreign-born Mexican-origin young people seen in Figures 8.1 and 8.2 probably reflect not only the fact that even young Mexican immigrants generally enter the United States seeking jobs, but also the socioeconomic and human capital disadvantages of Mexican immigrant families (on the latter, see Crosnoe, 2006). The undocumented status of many Mexican immigrant youth also has created difficulties for their pursuit of higher education. However, taking the multiple disadvantages of Mexican immigrant children into consideration, a substantial body of literature has supported seeing involvement in Mexican immigrant social circles as a positive contribution to school performance, and movement away from those social circles as a source of educational decline. Maria E. Matute-Bianchi (1986), for example, found in a study of California high school students that Mexican-descent children born in the United States often developed "a collective identity as a disadvantaged, disparaged minority group" (p. 255). Matute-Bianchi found that academic achievement among students of Mexican descent was often associated with avoiding the social circles of second- and third-generation "Cholos" and "Chicanos" in favor of Mexican-oriented peer groups and identity.

Since then, in a demographic study of the likelihood of high school completion among youth of Hispanic, Asian, and African immigrant background, Perreira et al. (2006) found that first-generation Asian and Hispanic young people generally obtain more education than their parents, but that second, third, and higher generations tend to lose ground. Similarly, the studies published in a more recent volume edited by Coll and Marks (2011) examine the "immigrant paradox"; that is, the common research finding that generations of immigrant children, including Hispanic immigrant children, experience diminishing developmental outcomes and educational achievements.

The immigrant paradox and generational decline take place within intergroup educational stratification. In other words, less assimilated generations of Mexican and other Hispanic students do better in school than more assimilated generations, but both tend to do less well than non-Hispanic white or Asian students. Within each Asian national origin group, moreover, school performance tends to be better among the less assimilated than the more assimilated, but there are clear differences among groups.

There seems to be, then, a general phenomenon of generational decline in education, associated with loosening ties to immigrant groups. If less advantaged groups constrain educational mobility in many ways, they also at least offer better options than those available to young people in the same disadvantaged segments of American society without access to immigrant social circles. At the other end of the ethnic stratification spectrum, descendants of immigrants who lose touch with the supports and pressures of professional immigrant networks will lose access to complementary social capital, so that the grandchildren of Asian Indian physicians or engineers, for example, can be expected to continue in the American middle class, without the same striking achievements as the earlier generation.

Min Zhou and I had an opportunity to examine generational decline in one location in American society, among the descendants of Vietnamese refugees. In a research project that we began in the early 1990s, we studied immigrant community influences on Vietnamese American young people. Based on our findings, we proposed a multi-level model of social integration in an immigrant ethnic network. We argued that individual young people are embedded in families and that these families are, further, embedded in multiple sets of social contexts and social relations. Moreover, the individuals and their families are located in particular neighborhoods and surrounded by local social environments where interpersonal relations are largely secondary and beyond ethnic boundaries. The consequences of moving out of an ethnic immigrant network and into a local social environment depend on what the local environment has to offer. In terms of the present discussion, leaving the network and becoming absorbed in the setting around it can be a matter of simply becoming a member of the middle class, for the children of professional immigrants, or becoming part of a much less advantageous environment.

The benefits of the network depend on its characteristics, as well as on what surrounds it. My co-author and I found that the Vietnamese young people we studied were tightly bound up in a system of social relations that provided both control and direction. As I have described earlier in the present work, the refugee adults were relatively new arrivals who placed great emphasis on striving for opportunities and expected young people to obtain these opportunities through the American educational system. As a result, adolescents who were closely connected to their communities through families and peer groups were directed in ways likely to pay off through school success. At the same time, though, young people who were not enmeshed in the Vietnamese community were not only more likely to become acculturated to a local social environment, in which delinquency and low achievement were common, but were also rejected by adult Vietnamese, who described the youthful non-conformists as "too Americanized." During the 1990s, Min Zhou and I predicted that network controls over young people would loosen over time and that more young people who remained in the community would show signs of low achievement and problematic behavior, and fewer would display the types of behavior associated with high performance in school (see Zhou and Bankston, 1994; 1998).

In a book chapter published in 2006, we reported the results of our follow-up study a decade later. At the beginning, we quoted the remarks of an instructor at a college in California, who said,

> It used to be that the Vietnamese were always the best in my classes. Any time I saw a Vietnamese name on my roster, I knew that person was going to be a star. Now, it isn't like that. I still get some good students who are Vietnamese, but a lot of them seem even worse than the others. And it's weird, because these kids today were all born here and speak good English. (Zhou and Bankston, 2006: 117)

My co-author and I remarked that these comments seemed to echo opinions we had heard from many professionals in education, law enforcement, and social services.

Based on surveys of attitudes, activities, and peer groups, in the 2006 study we found that more Vietnamese young people were falling into the cluster of those displaying problematic behavior and low achievement, and fewer were falling into the cluster associated with high achievement. Moreover, the respondents in general, but especially among those in the problematic cluster, were less strongly connected to the adult Vietnamese community and more acculturated to American society in general and to the local part of American society than were the youth we studied in the 1990s.

There is evidence, then, that immigrant networks can promote educational mobility to differing degrees for different groups, depending on network characteristics. As descendants of immigrants are absorbed into American society, connections to networks tend to become weaker, and those descendants lose the upward propulsion. The probable future is ironic for those who achieve fairly advantaged socioeconomic positions. The social ties help them move up and the upward movement weakens and ultimately dissolves the ties.

Even for young people in the Spanish-speaking working class, links to opportunity-seeking immigrants can be helpful, although the pay-off of these links is often limited by restricted information within the group and by fairly loose connections resulting from high geographic mobility and competition for jobs. The version of generational decline affecting these young people and their descendants is most likely to be absorption into hyper-segregated native-born American peer groups. This last point raises the question of whether some version of assimilation may, under some circumstances, be more advantageous than reliance on ethnic connections, given the limited social capital available within the networks and the dangers of acculturation into highly disadvantaged communities.

If the alternative to immigrant interpersonal ties consists mainly of highly isolated neighborhoods and schools, then the children of immigrants in groups such as North America's Mexicans will often find themselves in unenviable situations: limited social resources within their immigrant webs and less opportunity outside. If, on the other hand, they can obtain access to schools and contacts in more affluent settings, then they may indeed be able to receive resources beyond the financial, human, and social capital that the networks of the immigrant generation were able to provide.

Conclusion:
Networks, Social Capital,
and Immigrants

Social capital approaches usually use the forms of interpersonal networks to account for how people migrate and for the social and economic adaptation of immigrants. These approaches therefore raise the question of where those interpersonal networks come from. This book has attempted to answer that question by arguing that immigrants form their connections to each other in response to the conditions under which they leave their home countries and move to host countries. Network approaches to immigration, then, can be understood not as alternatives to traditional push–pull explanations, but as accounts of how those pushes and pulls work by shaping relationships among immigrants and between immigrants and natives.

The push and pull factors, further, operate within the context of connections between sending and receiving countries. Geographic proximity is one way in which countries are connected. It is relatively easy to move across boundaries in response to adverse conditions in one and labor demand in the other when nations are relatively close or adjoining. Neither proximity nor economics, though, accounts for who moves or the ways in which they move. Geographic proximity is just one among many ways in which countries may be connected in a manner that encourages large and highly flexible flows of labor, though. In some cases two countries may be closely connected due to a long history of recruiting by one in the other, combined with relatively easy transportation between the two. There are some parallels, for example, between the contemporary American Spanish-speaking working class, mainly from Mexico, and Germany's historic Turkish working class. In both cases, the locations of immigrants in the society and the economy result from a social proximity, in which immigrants have well-established socioeconomic positions. Geographic proximity and relations between sending and receiving countries can, in addition, influence characteristics of the internal structures of countries, such as country of origin institutions and economic specializations.

Historical geopolitical links can make possible more gradual and systematic, if continually increasing, migration along lines of official immigration policies. While all immigrants follow versions of chain migration, this type of gradual and systematic movement can encourage tighter interpersonal connections than usually exist among those who simply follow kin and neighbors across a permeable border in search of jobs. Tight interpersonal links among group members in a foreign land, combined with comparatively small group size, promotes concentration at the margins of the host country economy, especially in activities such as entrepreneurship. The tight network connections at the beginning of the migration process are maintained and furthered by this occupational concentration because this is how the immigrants adapt to their environment.

International and historic relations among countries may also result in the relatively sudden arrival of a large number of immigrants, as in the situations of some refugee influxes. This political version of push–pull factors tends to mean that network connections are less important for the process of international migration than such connections are for border crossers or visa seekers. Still, the suddenness of arrival often motivates these immigrants to settle or resettle in ethnic pockets.

While some forms of geographic or social proximity between nations may promote the movement of immigrants as a laboring class, other types of proximity can direct immigrants into underserved slots in more advantaged positions. Historic connections between nations that "pre-assimilate" potential immigrants by inculcating potential immigrants with familiarity with the receiving country and relevant skills can constitute this type of social proximity. In this case, immigrant networks may be less immediately visible, but they can still exist with their own distinctive forms and consequences.

Essentially, then, networks take shape within migration contexts; notably, economic and political push and pull factors and socioeconomic structures. Within the United States, I have pointed out the growth of low-wage labor and service positions and the growth of professional, high-skilled positions as the most notable structural feature. This is also arguably a dominant feature of other developed, migrant-receiving countries. The examples of immigrant networks that I have discussed in the previous pages do not exhaust the forms that social networks may take in response to contexts, but they can serve to illustrate how migration networks take shape.

The network forms can be considered at several different levels. Among these, family networks are especially important for the process of migration and for adaptation to life in the new homeland. The degree to which immigrant kinship patterns emphasize nuclear or extended families and patterns of relationships among family members depend on the roles that families play in migration and in fitting in to life in the receiving country. In turn, family connections provide different kinds of social assets in different immigrant groups.

Family networks exist within larger communities. I have categorized these larger communities as enclaves, neighborhoods, and communities in general. Enclaves, as I use the term in this book, describe the type of immigrant network most often considered in social capital research: close-knit, densely interconnected ethnic settlements characterized by strong social support and intense social control. Immigrant communities approximate enclaves to varying extents, depending on internal organization and links to the outside, as well as on amounts of cohesion. Moreover, a set of immigrants may show some characteristics of an enclave even in the absence of a single residential concentration, if the communication and interconnections usually associated with living together closely are present. Similarly, immigrants may live together in a neighborhood without high solidarity and close linkages. Communities in general exist whenever immigrants have social ties with each other beyond their immediate families. Even immigrant groups that are ostensibly "assimilated" in many respects may maintain ties, and these ties can provide social resources. The kinds of social resources available within all immigrant communities depend on their internal organization, their cohesion, and the information that can flow along network lines.

Networks, as sets of ties or as sources of information, exist among people and join groups of people, but formal institutions can be particularly important organizing components or means of focusing network relations. Although clubs, business, and civic organizations can enable immigrants to use their social resources, religious institutions are often especially central to immigrant interaction because of the power of religion to motivate and create solidarity. I have argued that the ability of religious institutions to turn interpersonal relations into assets depends heavily on how closely the institutions are bound to their underlying informal networks through active participation and control by members. A "strong institution" brings informal interpersonal connections into an organizational focus and can generate substantial trust, interdependence, and control. It can therefore be effective at channeling information and the flow of material resources.

The interlocking of multiple formal institutions is often associated with an enclave-type community, and interlocking institutions contribute to the capacity of immigrant enclaves to intensify social bonds and translate them into support, cooperation, and direction. Other types of immigrant communities that do not have the intense solidarity associated with enclaves can also turn interpersonal connections into resources through formal institutions, though. Symbolic associations, those that exist as expressions of group identity, can turn the idea of ethnicity itself into an asset for various types of communities by bringing people together in symbolically rich events and activities.

In speaking of family, community, and institutional networks and in considering networks as sources of assets for immigrants we are ultimately concerned with how these interpersonal arrangements result in adaptation. I have suggested that the fundamental forms of adaptation are economic and educational. Social capital for economic adaptation mainly concerns how immigrant networks affect occupations. Social capital for educational adaptation mainly concerns how networks affect academic achievement and attainment. The first considers primarily how social ties among members of an immigrant generation contribute to employment and economic well-being. The second considers how social ties affect intergenerational mobility for immigrant children and the descendants of immigrants.

Social networks shaped by structures of opportunity enable members of different ethnic groups to move into distinctive occupational concentrations, or ethnic specializations. Ties among individuals in immigrant groups channel information about opportunities and furnish support and control, thereby directing individuals to take advantage of opportunities. Links between immigrant group members and the larger society make some opportunities more readily available than others. I have referred to the two broad types of ethnic specializations as ethnic jobs and ethnic economies. The first term refers to occupations in which members of an ethnic group are heavily represented because their networks enable them to find and enter those occupations. I have used the term "ethnic economies," on the other hand, for networks that create economic opportunities out of immigrant social relations, most notably through entrepreneurship. Ethnic jobs can be found at the relatively low end of the socioeconomic scale and at the relatively high end, depending on how specific networks fit in to the job market. At the same time that these networks serve as resources for their members by creating access, they also restrict the occupational movement of their members and they exclude non-members. Most sizable groups have multiple specializations, which often intersect, and the specializations of different groups often connect in a pattern of ethnic stratification.

A network-based social capital approach to immigration can also help us understand how ethnic stratification perpetuates itself across generations. Social capital accounts of the educational achievement and attainment of immigrant children and children of immigrants usually place heavy emphasis on connections within families and on densely knit, relatively closed social networks. Intense bonding ties often are associated with scholastic performance because of the support, control, and direction that these types of ties can provide. I have argued that immigrant social capital can be conceptualized more broadly as all the different ways in which social relations among immigrants contribute to academic achievement among members of a younger generation. In general, the contributions may be compensatory or complementary. Compensatory social capital exists when immigrant interpersonal connections enable children from relatively disadvantaged groups to overcome challenges, especially the challenge of settlement in an underprivileged segment of American society. Complementary social capital exists when immigrant social networks enhance the abilities of professional or other relatively advantaged immigrants to pass on human capital.

Although relatively closed networks may promote educational mobility among some groups, particularly groups with a relatively short history in the host country, isolation from the surrounding society can also intensify "negative social capital." To understand how isolation can turn networks into means of perpetuating low academic achievement or attainment, one must look at the kinds of information that can be passed along network lines. A history of discrimination against members of a group, for example, can result in information about chances for life improvement that focuses on barriers to opportunity, rather than chances for opportunity.

Variations in network structure and in information within networks produce variations across groups in American schools. Nevertheless, immigrant groups in general do tend to be oriented toward mobility to some extent precisely because they leave one country and go to another in order to improve their lives. This mobility orientation is part of the social investment in children because immigrant social relations communicate messages of seeking opportunity to younger people. This communication raises the question of whether there is a tendency toward some sort of decline across generations as the networks that provide compensatory or complementary social capital loosen. In some situations, the decline may result in assimilation into the most alienated and disheartened segments of American society, as segmented assimilation theory has suggested. However, decline can mean different things for young people growing up in different locations in American society. It can mean the loss of already limited chances for educational mobility or it can mean simply a flattening out of achievement levels higher than those of most American students.

Although this discussion of how immigrant social networks can produce social capital has focused on immigration to the United States and has used four specific groups as its primary examples, its purpose has been to investigate the nature of immigrant networks and social capital in general, and to consider how networks provide the mechanisms by which social structures translate into variations in life experiences among immigrants as interconnected individuals. I want to suggest very briefly that seeing networks as resources can also address fundamental theoretical issues about human life. A network perspective can help us think not only about how individuals fit into social groups, but also about problems such as agency and structure.

In a brief summary of different approaches to agency and structure, George Ritzer (1992) describes "agency" as human action. Usually, this is a matter of individual actors, but it can also refer to collective actors, such as groups, organizations, nations, and even social classes. The term "structure" most often refers to large-scale social structures, but can also refer to small-scale patterns such as repeated interactions (1992: 568). I suggest that networks can account for how even collectivities such as ethnic groups can be seen as actors by focusing on the collaborative and reflexive decision making of individuals in response to social settings that results, for example, in labor market specializations.

Anthony Giddens's (1984) theory of "structuration" is probably the best-known effort to integrate agency and structure. Consistent with the idea that immigrant groups engage in collaborative and reflexive decision making among interconnected individuals, in Giddens's view actors continually order and reorder their practices in response to social structures and, in doing so, they create and reshape those structures. Vietnamese immigrants, finding themselves as newcomers at the margins of a service-oriented economy, began to find jobs in pedicure and manicure. Those in this field brought in other group members and, as they achieved some representation in the occupation, provided funds and labor that enabled them to transform this corner of the labor market into an ethnic niche and into a recognizable part of the beauty industry. Their occupational concentration, in turn, shaped their own decision making about jobs and reordered their social networks.

Finally, network approaches to immigration and immigrant adaptation have important policy implications. Understanding how immigrants function in a society and in an economy requires close study of immigrant groups as distinctive sets of interacting members. They are not simply individuals or categories. If the goal of policy is to address socioeconomic or educational disparities among groups, then policy will need to develop sensitivity to variations in interactions within and across groups. Simply put, policies that may address the needs of Korean or Vietnamese immigrants and their children may not address the needs of Mexican or Guatemalan children (or vice versa), and comprehending these needs goes beyond descriptions of national cultures. Since immigrants act through their interpersonal networks, recognition of networks should be central to policies regarding immigrants.

References

Acacio, Kristel. 2007. "Rethinking Supply Side Factors: The Role of Formal Organizations and Institutions in Philippine Nurse Migration." Unpublished paper presented at the annual meetings of the American Sociological Association.

Aguilera, Michael B., and Douglas S. Massey. 2003. "Social Capital and the Wages of Mexican Migrants: New Hypotheses and Tests." *Social Forces* 82: 671–701.

Airriess, Christopher A., Wei Li, Karen J. Leong, Angela Chia-Chen Chen, and Verna M. Keith. 2008. "Church-Based Social Capital, Networks, and Geographical Scale: Katrina Evacuation, Relocation, and Recovery in a New Orleans Vietnamese Community." *Geoforum* 39: 1333–46.

Alba, Richard, John Logan, and Kyle Crowder. 1997. "White Neighborhoods and Assimilation: The Greater New York Region, 1980–1990." *Social Forces* 75: 883–909.

Almeida, Joanna, Ichiro Kawachi, Beth E. Molnar, and S.V. Subramanian. 2009. "A Multilevel Analysis of Social Ties and Social Cohesion among Latinos and their Neighbors: Results from Chicago." *Journal of Urban Health* 5: 745–59.

Ashton, Gayle. 1985 (Apr. 21). "Shrimping: A Small Revolution on the Water." *Times-Picayune*, section A, p. 13.

Bankston, Carl L. III. 1990. "Landfill in the Bayou: An Environmental Protest Movement in the New Orleans Vietnamese Community." *The Progressive* 54(July): 8–9.

Bankston, Carl L. III. 1995. "Gender Roles and Scholastic Performance Among Adolescent Vietnamese Women: The Paradox of Ethnic Patriarchy." *Sociological Focus* 28: 161–76.

Bankston, Carl L. III. 1996. "Edge Village: The Suburban Ecology of a Laotian Community." Presented at the annual meetings of the Mid-South Sociological Association, Little Rock, Arkansas.

References

Bankston, Carl L. III. 1997. "Bayou Lotus: Theravada Buddhism in Southwestern Louisiana." *Sociological Spectrum* 17: 453–72.

Bankston, Carl L. III. 2000. "Sangha of the South: Laotian Buddhism and Social Adaptation in Southwestern Louisiana." Pp. 357–71 in *Contemporary Asian America* (1st edition), edited by Min Zhou and James V. Gatewood. Albany: New York University Press.

Bankston, Carl L. III. 2006. "Filipino Americans." Pp. 180–203 in *Asian Americans: Contemporary Issues and Trends* (2nd edition), edited by Pyong Gap Min. Thousand Oaks: Pine Forge Press.

Bankston, Carl L. III. 2009a. "The Building and Rebuilding of La Nueva Orleans." Unpublished paper presented to the 27th Annual Journalists and Editors Workshop, sponsored by Florida International University.

Bankston, Carl L. III. 2009b. "Hispanic New Orleans: Origins and Prospects." Unpublished paper presented at the annual meetings of the Mid-South Sociological Association, Lafayette, Louisiana.

Bankston, Carl L. III. 2009c. "The Rise of the Rest Inside the U.S.: The Global Economic Setting and American Immigration in a Post-American World." *International Review of Modern Sociology* 35: 181–204.

Bankston, Carl L. III. 2012a. "Disaster and Demographics: Hurricanes, Immigration, and Ethnic Stratification in New Orleans." Unpublished paper presented at the Southern Sociology in the 21st Century Conference, Louisiana State University.

Bankston, Carl L. 2012b. "The International Immigrants of Mississippi: An Overview." Pp. 15–31 in *Ethnic Heritage in Mississippi: The Twentieth Century*, edited by Shana Walton. Jackson: University Press of Mississippi.

Bankston, Carl L. III. 2012c. "The Limits of Desegregation Policy and Constructive Alternatives in the Face of Resegregation." Unpublished paper presented at the annual meeting of the Southern Sociological Society, New Orleans, Louisiana.

Bankston, Carl L. III. Forthcoming(a). "Cambodian Americans." In *Gale Encyclopedia of Multicultural America* (3rd edition).

Bankston, Carl L. III. Forthcoming(b). "Vietnamese Americans." In *Gale Encyclopedia of Multicultural America* (3rd edition).

Bankston, Carl L. III., and Stephen J. Caldas. 1996. "Adolescents and Deviance in a Vietnamese American Community: A Theoretical Synthesis." *Deviant Behavior* 17: 159–81.

Bankston, Carl L. III., and Min Zhou. 1996. "Go Fish: The Louisiana Vietnamese and Ethnic Entrepreneurship in an Extractive Industry." *National Journal of Sociology* 10: 37–55.

Bankston, Carl L. III., and Min Zhou. 1997. "Valedictorians and Delinquents: The Bifurcation of Vietnamese American Youth." *Deviant Behavior* 18: 343–63.

References

Bankston, Carl L. III., and Min Zhou. 2002. "Social Capital as Process: The Meanings and Problems of a Theoretical Metaphor." *Sociological Inquiry* 72: 285–317.

Bastida, Elena. 2001. "Kinship Ties of Mexican Migrant Women on the United States/Mexico Border." *Journal of Comparative Family Studies* 32: 549–69.

Bellah, Robert. 1970. *Beyond Belief: Essays on Religion in a Post-Traditional World.* New York: Harper & Row.

Berger, Joseph. 2003 (Nov. 24). "From the Philippines, With Scrubs: How One Ethnic Group Came to Dominate the Nursing Field." *New York Times*, p. B1.

Beveridge, Andrew A. 2002. "Immigrant Residence and Immigrant Neighborhoods in New York, 1910 and 1990." Pp. 199–230 in *Mass Migration to the United States*, edited by Andrew A. Beveridge. Walnut Creek: Altamira Press.

Blau, Peter. 1977. *Inequality and Heterogeneity.* New York: Free Press.

Blau, Peter, and Joseph Schwartz. 1984. *Crosscutting Social Circles.* New York: Academic Press.

Blau, Peter M., Carolyn Beeker, and Kevin M. Fitzpatrick. 1984. "Intersecting Social Affiliations and Intermarriage." *Social Forces* 62: 585–606.

Blau, Peter M., Terry C. Blum, and Joseph E. Schwartz. 1982. "Heterogeneity and Intermarriage." *American Sociological Review* 47: 45–62.

Bonacich, Edna, and J. Modell. 1980. *The Economic Basis of Ethnic Solidarity: Small Business in the Japanese American Community.* Berkeley: University of California Press.

Bonus, R. 2000. *Locating Filipino Americans: Ethnicity and the Cultural Politics of Space.* Philadelphia: Temple University Press.

Bourdieu, Pierre. 1985. "The Forms of Capital." Pp. 241–58 in *Handbook of Theory and Research in the Sociology of Education*, edited by J.G. Richardson. New York: Greenwood Press.

Brashears, Matthew. 2010. "Anomia and the Sacred Canopy: Testing a Network Theory." *Social Networks* 32: 187–96.

Brettell, Caroline B. 2005. "Voluntary Organizations, Social Capital, and the Social Incorporation of Asian Indian Immigrants in the Dallas–Fort Worth Metroplex." *Anthropological Quarterly* 78: 853–83.

Brint, Steven. 2001. "*Gemeinschaft* Revisited: A Critique and Reconstruction of the Community Concept." *Sociological Theory* 19: 1–23.

Brooke, Bob. 1999. "Community Organizations Revitalize Latino Neighborhoods." *Hispanic* 13(4): 56.

Broom, J. 2003 (Dec. 14). "Filipinos Who Paved the Way. Two Photo Exhibits Chronicle an Immigrant Community." *Seattle Times*, p. L1.

Campion, Patricia. 2003. "One Under God? A Baptist Mission Ministering to Immigrants in Southern Louisiana." *Sociological Spectrum* 23: 279–301.

191

References

Caplan, Nathan, Marcella H. Choy, and John K. Whitmore. 1989. *The Boat People and Achievement in America: A Study of Family Life, Hard Work, and Cultural Values.* Ann Arbor: University of Michigan Press.

Caplan, Nathan, Marcella H. Choy, and John K. Whitmore. 1991. *Children of the Boat People.* Ann Arbor: University of Michigan Press.

Caplan, Nathan, John K. Whitmore, and Marcella H. Choy. 1992. "Indochinese Refugee Families and Academic Achievement." *Scientific American* 266(February): 36–42.

Chávez, L.R. 1985. "Households, Migration and Labor Market Participation: The Adaptation of Mexicans to Life in the United States." *Urban Anthropology* 14: 301–45.

Chávez, L.R. 1990. "Coresidence and Resistance: Strategies for Survival among Undocumented Mexicans and Central Americans in the U.S." *Urban Anthropology* 19: 31–61.

Chávez, Maria L., Brian Wampler, and Ross E. Burkhart. 2006. "Left Out: Trust and Social Capital Among Migrant Seasonal Farmworkers." *Social Science Quarterly* 87: 1012–29.

Child, Irving. 1943. *Italian or American: The Second Generation in Conflict.* New Haven: Yale University Press.

Choy, Catherine Ceniza. 2003. *Empire of Care: Nursing and Migration in Filipino American History.* Durham: Duke University Press.

Coleman, James S. 1988. "Social Capital in the Creation of Human Capital." *American Sociological Review* 94: S95–S120.

Coleman, James S. 1990. *Foundations of Social Theory.* Cambridge: Belknap Press of Harvard University Press.

Coll, Cynthia Garcia, and Amy Kerivan Marks, eds. 2011. *The Immigrant Paradox in Children and Adolescents: Is Becoming American a Developmental Risk?* Washington, D.C.: APA Books.

Crosnoe, Robert. 2006. *Mexican Roots, American Schools: Helping Mexican Immigrant Children Succeed.* Palo Alto: Stanford University Press.

Dao, Vy. n.d. *Deeply Southern: A Qualitative Study of Community, Disaster, and Settlement of Vietnamese Americans along the Gulf Coast.* Ph.D. dissertation in preparation, Tulane University.

David-Barrett, Tamas, and R.I.M. Dunbar. 2012. "Cooperation, Behavioral Synchrony and Status in Social Networks." *Journal of Theoretical Biology* 308: 88–95.

De Jong, Gordon F., Brenda Davis Root, and Ricardo G. Abad. 1986. "Family Reunification and Philippine Migration to the United States: The Immigrants' Perspective." *International Migration Review* 20: 598–611.

Del Pozo, Monica, Conrado Manuel, Enrique Gonzalez-Araguena, and Guillermo Owen. 2011. "Centrality in Directed Social Networks: A Game Theoretic Approach." *Social Networks* 33: 191–200.

Dhingra, Pawan. 2010. "Hospitable to Others: Indian American Hotel Owners

References

Create Boundaries and Belonging in the Heartland." *Ethnic and Racial Studies* 33: 1088–107.

Dhingra, Pawan. 2012. *Life Behind the Lobby: Indian American Motel Owners and the American Dream*. Palo Alto: Stanford University Press.

Donato, Katharine M., and Evelyn Patterson. 2004. "Men and Women on the Move: Undocumented Border Crossing." Pp. 111–30 in *Crossing the Border: Research from the Mexican Migration Project*, edited by Jorge Durand and Douglas S. Massey. New York: Russell Sage Foundation.

Donato, Katharine M., and Carl L. Bankston III. 2008. "The Origins of Employer Demand for Immigrants in a New Destination: The Salience of Soft Skills in a Volatile Economy." Pp. 124–48 in *New Faces in New Places: The Changing Geography of American Immigration*, edited by Douglas S. Massey. New York: Russell Sage Foundation.

Donato, Katharine M., Carl L. Bankston III, and Dawn T. Robinson. 2001. "Immigration and the Organization of the Onshore Oil Industry: Southern Louisiana in the Late 1990s." Pp. 105–13 in *Latino Workers in the Contemporary South*, edited by Arthur D. Murphy, Colleen Blanchard, and Jennifer A. Hill. Athens: University of Georgia Press.

Donato, Katharine M., Melissa Stainbeck, and Carl L. Bankston III. 2005. "The Economic Incorporation of Mexican Immigrants in South Louisiana: A Tale of Two Cities." Pp. 76–99 in *New Destinations of Mexican Immigration in the United States*, edited by Victor Zúñiga and Rubén Hernández-León. New York: Russell Sage Foundation.

Donato, Katharine M., Nicole Trujillo-Pagán, Carl L. Bankston III, and Audrey Singer. 2010. "Immigration, Reconstruction and Settlement: Hurricane Katrina and the Emergence of Immigrant Communities." Pp. 265–90 in *The Sociology of Katrina* (2nd edition), edited by David L. Brunsma, David Overfelt, and J. Steven Picou. New York: Rowman & Littlefield.

Doreian, Patrick, and Norman Conti. 2012. "Social Context, Spatial Structure and Social Network Structure." *Social Networks* 34: 32–46.

Ebaugh, Helen Rose, and Janet Saltzman Chafetz, eds. 2000. *Religion and the New Immigrants: Continuities and Adaptations in Immigrant Congregations*. Walnut Creek: Altamira Press.

Eng, Sothy, Kirti Kanitkar, Harrison H. Cleveland, Richard Herbert, Judith Fischer, and Jacqueline D. Wiersma. 2008. "School Achievement Differences among Chinese and Filipino American Students: Acculturation and the Family." *Educational Psychology* 28: 535–50.

Esses, Victoria M., John F. Dovidio, Lynne M. Jackson, and Tamara L. Armstrong. 2001. "The Immigration Dilemma: The Role of Perceived Group Competition, Ethnic Prejudice, and National Identity." *Journal of Social Issues* 57: 389–412.

Feld, Scott L. 1981. "The Focused Organization of Social Ties." *American Journal of Sociology* 86: 1015–35.

References

Feliciano, Cynthia. 2006. "Beyond the Family: The Influence of Premigration Group Status on the Educational Expectations of Immigrants' Children." *Sociology of Education* 79: 281–303.

Fernández Kelly, M. Patricia. 1995. "Social and Cultural Capital in the Urban Ghetto: Implications for the Economic Sociology of Immigration." Pp. 213–47 in *The Economic Sociology of Immigration*, edited by Alejandro Portes. New York: Russell Sage Foundation.

Fernández Kelly, M. Patricia. 2002. "Commentary: Uses and Misuses of Social Capital." Pp. 73–84 in *Schooling and Social Capital in Diverse Cultures*, edited by Bruce Fuller and Emily Hannum. Amsterdam: Elsevier Science.

Flores-Yeffal, Nadia Y., and Maria Aysa-Lastra. 2011. "Place of Origin, Types of Ties, and Support Networks in Mexico–U.S. Migration." *Rural Sociology* 76: 481–510.

Flynn, Francis J., Ray E. Reagans, and Lucia Guillory. 2010. "Do You Two Know Each Other? Transitivity, Homophily, and the Need for (Network) Closure." *Journal of Personality and Social Psychology* 99: 855–69.

Fry, Richard, and Paul Taylor. 2012. *Hispanic High School Graduates Pass Whites in Rate of College Enrollment*. Washington, D.C.: Pew Hispanic Center.

Fukuyama, Francis. 1999. *The Great Disruption: Human Nature and the Reconstitution of Social Order*. New York: Free Press.

Gans, Herbert J. 1979. "Symbolic Ethnicity: The Future of Ethnic Groups and Cultures in America." *Ethnic and Racial Studies* 2: 1–20.

Gans, Herbert J. 1992. "Second Generation Decline: Scenarios for the Economic and Ethnic Futures of the Post-1965 American Immigrants." *Ethnic and Racial Studies* 15: 173–92.

Garcia, Carlos. 2005. "*Buscando Trabajo*: Social Networking among Immigrants from Mexico to the United States." *Hispanic Journal of Behavioral Sciences* 27: 3–22.

Gellis, Zvu D. 2003. "Kin and Nonkin Social Supports in a Community Sample of Vietnamese Immigrants." *Social Work* 48: 248–58.

Giddens, Anthony. 1984. *The Constitution of Society: Outline of the Theory of Structuration*. Cambridge: Polity.

Gordon, Milton M. 1964. *Assimilation in American Life: The Role of Race, Religion, and National Origins*. New York: Oxford University Press.

Goyette, Kimberly A., and Gilberto Q. Conchas. 2002. "Family and Non-Family Roots of Social Capital among Vietnamese and Mexican American Children." Pp. 41–72 in *Schooling and Social Capital in Diverse Cultures*, edited by Bruce Fuller and Emily Hannum. Amsterdam: Elsevier Science.

Granovetter, Mark. 1973. "The Strength of Weak Ties." *American Journal of Sociology* 78: 1360–80.

Grayson, James H. 2009. "The Emplantation of Christianity: An Anthropological Examination of the Korean Church." *Transformation* 26: 161–73.

References

Guthey, Greig. 2001. "Mexican Places in Southern Spaces: Globalization, Work, and Daily Life in and around the North Georgia Poultry Industry." Pp. 57–67 in *Latino Workers in the Contemporary South*, edited by Arthur D. Murphy, Colleen Blanchard, and Jennifer A. Hill. Athens: University of Georgia Press.

Harris, Angel L., Kenneth M. Jamison, and Monica H. Trujillo. 2008. "Disparities in the Educational Success of Immigrants: An Assessment of the Immigrant Effect for Asians and Latinos." *Annals of the American Academy of Political and Social Science* 620: 90–114.

Hein, Jeremy. 1995. *From Vietnam, Laos, and Cambodia: A Refugee Experience in the United States*. New York: Twayne.

Hernández-León, Rubén. 2007. "Review Symposium" (by Rubén Hernández-León, Peter Kivisto, and Roger Waldinger, with response by Ivan Light). *Ethnic and Racial Studies* 30: 1152–6.

Hernández-León, Rubén, and Victor Zúñiga. 2000. "Making Carpet by the Mile: The Emergence of a Mexican Immigrant Community in an Industrial Region of the U.S. Historic South." *Social Science Quarterly* 81: 49–66.

Hernández-León, Rubén, and Victor Zúñiga. 2003. "Mexican Immigrant Communities in the South and Social Capital: The Case of Dalton, Georgia." *Southern Rural Sociology* 19: 20–45.

Hernández-León, Rubén, and Victor Zúñiga. 2006. "Appalachia Meets Aztlán: Mexican Immigration and Intergroup Relations in Dalton, Georgia." Pp. 244–75 in *New Destinations: Mexican Immigration in the United States*, edited by Victor Zúñiga and Rubén Hernández-León. New York: Russell Sage Foundation.

Hidalgo, Danielle Antoinette, and Carl L. Bankston III. 2008. "War Brides and Refugees: Vietnamese American Wives and Shifting Links to the Military, 1980–2000." *International Migration* 46: 199–217.

Hidalgo, Danielle Antoinette, and Carl L. Bankston III. 2011. "The Demilitarization of Thai American Marriage Migration, 1980–2000." *Journal of International Migration and Integration* 12: 85–99.

Hirschman, Charles, and Douglas S. Massey. 2008. "People and Places: The New American Mosaic." Pp. 1–21 in *New Faces in New Places: The Changing Geography of American Immigration*, edited by Douglas S. Massey. New York: Russell Sage Foundation.

Hirschman, Charles, and Morrison Wong. 1986. "The Extraordinary Educational Attainment of Asian-Americans: A Search for Historical Evidence and Explanations." *Social Forces* 65: 1–27.

Hitchcox, Linda. 1988. *Vietnamese Refugees in Process: Transit and Change*. Unpublished Ph.D. dissertation, Oxford University.

Hoefer, Michael, Nancy Rytina, and Bryan Baker. 2011. *Estimates of the Unauthorized Immigrant Population Residing in the United States: January, 2010*. Washington, D.C.: Department of Homeland Security, Office of Immigration Statistics.

Huerta, Alvaro. 2007. "Looking Beyond 'Mow, Blow, and Go': A Case Study of Mexican Immigrant Gardeners in Los Angeles." *Berkeley Planning Journal* 20: 1–23.

Iglic, Hajdeja. 2010. "Voluntary Associations and Tolerance: An Ambiguous Relationship." *American Behavioral Scientist* 53: 717–36.

Kao, Grace. 2004. "Social Capital and Its Relevance to Minority and Immigrant Populations." *Sociology of Education* 77: 172–5.

Kao, Grace, and Lindsay Taggart Rutherford. 2007. "Does Social Capital Still Matter? Immigrant Minority Disadvantage in School-Specific Social Capital and Its Effects on Academic Achievement." *Sociological Perspectives* 50: 27–52.

Karlan, Dean, Markus Mobius, Tanya Rosenblat, and Adam Szeidl. 2009. "Trust and Social Collateral." *Quarterly Journal of Economics* 124: 1307–61.

Kaushal, Neeraj, Cordelia W. Reimers, and David M. Reimers. 2008. "Immigrants and the Economy." Pp. 176–88 in *New Faces in New Places: The Changing Geography of American Immigration*, edited by Douglas S. Massey. New York: Russell Sage Foundation.

Kibria, Nazli. 1993. *Family Tightrope: The Changing Lives of Vietnamese Americans*. Princeton: Princeton University Press.

Kim, Dae Young. 2006. "Stepping Stone to Intergenerational Mobility? The Springboard, Safety Net, or Mobility Trap Functions of Korean Immigrant Entrepreneurship for the Second Generation." *International Migration Review* 40: 927–62.

Kim, Eun-Young. 1993. "Career Choice among Second-Generation Korean Americans: Reflections on a Cultural Model of Success." *Anthropology and Education Quarterly* 24: 224–48.

Kim, Eunjung. 2002. "The Relationship Between Parental Involvement and Children's Educational Achievement in the Korean Immigrant Family." *Journal of Comparative Family Studies* 33(4): 529–40.

Kim, Queena Sook. 2003 (Jan. 8). "Fate of Faded Ambassador Hotel Divides Korean Groups." *Wall Street Journal*, p. B1.

Kim, Rebecca Y. 2012. "Revival and Renewal: Korean American Protestants Beyond Immigrant Enclaves." *Studies in World Christianity* 18: 291–312.

Kwon, Victoria Hyonchu. 1997. *Entrepreneurship and Religion: Korean Immigrants in Houston, Texas*. New York: Garland.

Kwon, Victoria Hyonchu, Helen Rose Ebaugh, and Jacqueline Hagan. 1997. "The Structure and Functions of Cell Group Ministry in an American Korean Church." *Journal for the Scientific Study of Religion* 36: 247–56.

Lancee, Bram. 2012. "The Economic Returns of Bonding and Bridging Social Capital for Immigrant Men in Germany." *Ethnic and Racial Studies* 35: 664–83.

Lazo, Luz. 2012 (Jul. 18). "Nails Expert is Rising Leader among Vietnamese Americans." *Pittsburgh Post-Gazette*, p. A6.

References

Lee, Jennifer. 1999. "Retail Niche Domination among African American, Korean, and Jewish Entrepreneurs: Competition, Coethnic Advantage and Disadvantage." *American Behavioral Scientist* 42: 1398–416.

Lichter, Daniel. 2010. "Residential Segregation in New Hispanic Destinations: Cities, Suburbs, and Rural Communities Compared." *Social Science Research* 39: 215–30.

Light, Ivan. 2006. *Deflecting Immigration: Networks, Markets, and Regulation in Los Angeles.* New York: Russell Sage Foundation.

Light, Ivan, Richard B. Bernard, and Rebecca Kim. 1999. "Immigrant Incorporation in the Garment Industry of Los Angeles." *International Migration Review* 33: 5–25.

Lin, Nan. 1999. "Social Networks and Status Attainment." *Annual Review of Sociology* 25: 467–87.

Liu, John M., Paul M. Ong, and Carolyn Rosenstein. 1991. "Dual-Chain Migration: Post-1965 Filipino Immigration to the United States." *International Migration Review* 25: 487–513.

Loury, Glenn C. 1977. "A Dynamic Theory of Racial Income Differences." Pp. 153–86 in *Women, Minorities, and Employment Discrimination*, edited by Phyllis A. Wallace and Annette LaMond. Lexington: Heath.

Macatuno, E. 2002 (Oct.). "Our Town." *Filipinas Magazine*, pp. 71–2.

Manago, Dinorah. 2007. "Praying for Community: Faith-Based Community Organizations and Latino Immigrant Day Laborers." Unpublished paper presented at the annual meetings of the American Sociological Association, New York.

Martinez, Cid Gregory. 2009. "The Transformation of a Los Angeles Ghetto: Latino Immigration and the New Urban Social Order." *Dissertation Abstracts International* 70: 1439.

Massey, Douglas S. 1981. "Dimensions of the New Immigration to the United States and the Prospects for Assimilation." *Annual Review of Sociology* 7: 57–85.

Massey, Douglas S. 2007. *Categorically Unequal: The American Stratification System.* New York: Russell Sage Foundation.

Massey, Douglas S., and Chiara Capoferro. 2008. "The Geographic Diversification of Mexican Migration to New Destinations in the United States." Pp. 25–50 in *New Faces in New Places: The Changing Geography of American Immigration*, edited by Douglas S. Massey. New York: Russell Sage Foundation.

Massey, Douglas S., Luis Goldring, and Jorge Durand. 1994. "Continuities in Transnational Migration: An Analysis of Nineteen Mexican Communities." *American Journal of Sociology* 99: 1492–533.

Matute-Bianchi, Maria E. 1986. "Ethnic Identities and Patterns of School Success and Failure among Mexican-Descent and Japanese American Students in a California High School: An Ethnographic Analysis." *American Journal of Education* 93: 233–55.

References

Matute-Bianchi, Maria E. 1991. "Situational Ethnicity and Patterns of School Performance among Immigrant and Non-Immigrant Mexican-Descent Students." Pp. 205–47 in *Minority Status and Schooling: A Comparative Study of Immigrant and Involuntary Minorities*, edited by Margaret A. Gibson and John U. Ogbu. New York: Garland.

McDonald, Steve. 2011. "What's in the 'Old Boys' Network? Accessing Social Capital in Gendered and Racialized Networks." *Social Networks* 33: 317–30.

Menjívar, Cecilia. 2000. *Fragmented Ties: Salvadoran Immigrant Networks in America*. Berkeley: University of California Press.

Min, Pyong Gap. 1984. "An Exploratory Study of Kin Ties among Korean Immigrant Families in Atlanta." *Journal of Comparative Family Studies* 15: 59–75.

Min, Pyong Gap. 1992. "The Structure and Functions of Korean Immigrant Churches in the United States." *International Migration Review* 26: 1370–94.

Min, Pyong Gap. 1996. "Korean Americans." Pp. 230–59 in *Asian Americans: Contemporary Trends and Issues* (2nd edition), edited by Pyong Gap Min. Thousand Oaks: Pine Forge Press.

Nee, Victor, and H. Wong. 1985. "Asian American Socioeconomic Achievement: The Strength of the Family Bond." *Sociological Perspectives* 28: 281–306.

Ness, Immanuel. 2005. *Immigrant Unions and the New US Labor Market*. Philadelphia: Temple University Press.

Newberger, R., S.L.W. Rhine, and S. Chiu. 2004. *Immigrant Financial Market Participation: Defining Research Questions*. Chicago: Federal Reserve Bank of Chicago.

Odem, Mary E. 2004. "Our Lady of Guadalupe in the New South: Latin American Immigrants and the Politics of Integration in the Catholic Church." *Journal of American Ethnic History* 23: 29–60.

Oh, Joong-Hwan. 2007. "Economic Incentive, Embeddedness, and Social Support: A Study of Korean-Owned Nail Salon Workers' Rotating Credit Associations." *International Migration Review* 42: 623–55.

Oh, Sookhee. 2007. "Immigrant Communities and Consumption Linkages: Suburban Koreans in New Jersey." Unpublished paper presented at the annual meetings of the American Sociological Association, New York.

Pan, Ying. 2012. "The Impact of Legal Status on Immigrants' Earnings and Human Capital: Evidence from the IRCA 1986." *Journal of Labor Research* 33: 119–42.

Park, Jisung, Soonhee Roh, and Younsook Yeo. 2012. "Religiosity, Social Support, and Life Satisfaction among Elderly Korean Immigrants." *Gerontologist* 52: 641–9.

Park, Robert E. 1928. "Human Migration and the Marginal Man." *American Journal of Sociology* 33: 881–93.

References

Park, Robert E., R.D. Mackenzie, and Ernest Burgess. 1925. *The City: Suggestions for the Study of Human Nature*. Chicago: University of Chicago Press.

Park, Yoosun, Joshua Miller, and Bao Chau Van. 2010. "'Everything Has Changed': Narratives of the Vietnamese Community in Post-Katrina Mississippi." *Journal of Sociology & Social Welfare* 37: 79–105.

Patacsil, N. Judy. 2008. "Kapwa – Embracing Our Shared Identity: The Influence of Role Models on Being Filipino American." *Dissertation Abstracts International* 68: 7713–15.

Patel, Purva. 2005 (Apr. 29). "The Fall of Saigon 30 Years Later – Where the East Meets the West – Vietnamese-Americans Prosper by Serving Houston's Diversity." *Houston Chronicle*, Business Section, p. 1.

Paulson, A., A. Singer, R. Newberger, and J. Smith. 2006. *Financial Access for Immigrants: Lessons from Diverse Perspectives*. Chicago: Federal Reserve Bank of Chicago and the Brookings Institution.

Perreira, Krista M., Kathleen Mullan Harris, and Dohoon Lee. 2006. "Making It in America: High School Completion by Immigrant and Native Youth." *Demography* 43: 511–36.

Pew Hispanic Center. 2007. *Construction Jobs Expand for Latinos Despite Slump in Housing Market*, fact sheet. http://pewhispanic.org/factsheets/factsheet.php?FactsheetID=28

Pih, Kay Kei-Ho, Mario De La Rosa, Douglas Rugh, and Kuoray Mao. 2008. "Different Strokes for Different Gangs? An Analysis of Capital among Latino and Asian Gang Members." *Sociological Perspectives* 51: 473–94.

Portes, Alejandro. 1981. "Modes of Structural Incorporation and Present Theories of Labor Immigration." Pp. 279–97 in *Global Trends in Migration*, edited by Mary Kritz, Charles B. Keeley, and Silvano Tomasi. New York: Center for Migration Studies.

Portes, Alejandro. 1987. "The Social Origins of the Cuban Enclave in Miami." *Sociological Perspectives* 30: 340–72.

Portes, Alejandro. 1998. "Social Capital: Its Origins and Applications in Modern Sociology." *Annual Review of Sociology* 24: 1–24.

Portes, Alejandro, and Leif Jensen. 1987. "What's an Ethnic Enclave? The Case for Conceptual Clarity." *American Sociological Review* 52: 768–71.

Portes, Alejandro, and Leif Jensen. 1992. "Disproving the Enclave Hypothesis: Reply." *American Sociological Review* 57: 418–20.

Portes, Alejandro, and Robert Manning. 1986. "The Immigrant Enclave: Theory and Empirical Examples." Pp. 47–68 in *Comparative Ethnic Relations*, edited by Susan Olzak and Joanne Nagel. New York: Academic Press.

Portes, Alejandro, and J. Sensenbrenner. 1993. "Embeddedness and Immigration: Notes on the Social Determinants of Economic Action." *American Journal of Sociology* 98: 1320–50.

Posadas, Barbara M. 1999. *The Filipino Americans*. Westport: Greenwood Press.

References

Putnam, Robert D. 1993. "The Prosperous Community: Social Capital and Community Life." *American Prospect* 13(4): 35–42.

Putnam, Robert D. 1995. "Bowling Alone: America's Declining Social Capital." *Journal of Democracy* 6: 65–78.

Putnam, Robert D. 2000. *Bowling Alone: The Collapse and Revival of American Community*. New York: Simon & Schuster.

Putnam, Robert D. 2007. "*E Pluribus Unum*: Diversity and Community in the Twenty-First Century." *Scandinavian Political Studies* 30: 137–74.

Ramirez, Hernan, and Pierette Hondagneu-Sotelo. 2009. "Mexican Immigrant Gardeners: Entrepreneurs or Exploited Workers?" *Social Problems* 56: 70–88.

Ream, Robert K., and Russell W. Rumberger. 2008. "Student Engagement, Peer Social Capital, and School Dropout among Mexican-American and Non-Latino Students." *Sociology of Education* 81: 109–39.

Reimers, David M. 1985. *Still the Golden Door: The Third World Comes to America*. New York: Columbia University Press.

Rhine, S.L.W., and W.H. Greene. 2006. "The Determinants of Being Unbanked for U.S. Immigrants." *Journal of Consumer Affairs* 40: 21–40.

Ritzer, George. 1992. *Sociological Theory* (3rd edition). New York: McGraw-Hill.

Rodriguez, Nestor. 2004. "Workers Wanted: Employer Recruitment of Immigrant Labor." *Work and Occupations* 31: 453–73.

Ruggles, Steven J., Trent Alexander, Katie Genadek, Ronald Goeken, Matthew B. Schroeder, and Matthew Sobek. 2010. *Integrated Public Use Microdata Series: Version 5.0* [machine-readable database]. Minneapolis: University of Minnesota.

Rumbaut, Rubén G. 1994. "Origins and Destinies: Immigration to the United States Since World War II." *Sociological Forum* 4: 583–621.

Rutledge, Paul J. 1985. *The Role of Religion in Ethnic Self-Identity: A Vietnamese Community*. Lanham: University Press of America.

Ryan, Louise. 2011. "Migrants' Social Networks and Weak Ties: Accessing Resources and Constructing Relationships Post-Migration." *Sociological Review* 59: 707–24.

Saenz, Rogelio, and Carlos Siordia. 2012. "The Inter-Cohort Reproduction of Mexican-American Dropouts." *Race and Social Problems* 4: 68–81.

Sakamoto, Arthur, and Yu Xie. 2006. "The Socioeconomic Attainments of Asian Americans." Pp. 54–77 in *Asian Americans: Contemporary Issues and Trends* (2nd edition), edited by Pyong Gap Min. Thousand Oaks: Pine Forge Press.

Sampson, Robert J. 2012. *Great American City: Chicago and the Enduring Neighborhood Effect*. Chicago: University of Chicago Press.

Sanchirico, A. 1991. "The Importance of Small Business Ownership in Chinese American Educational Achievement." *Sociology of Education* 64: 293–304.

Sanders, Jimmy, and Victor Nee. 1987. "Limits of Ethnic Solidarity in the Enclave Economy." *American Sociological Review* 52: 745–67.

References

Schlifstein, Mark. 1988 (Dec. 3). "Fishing for Business." *Times-Picayune*, section A, p. 1.

Sisk, Blake, and Carl L. Bankston III. 2012. "A Construction Boom and a Disposable Labor Force: Hispanic Workers in Post-Katrina New Orleans." Unpublished paper presented at the annual meetings of the Southern Sociological Society, New Orleans, Louisiana.

Skoretz, John, and Filip Agneesens. 2007. "Reciprocity, Multiplexity, and Exchange Measures." *Quality & Quantity* 41: 341–57.

Smith, James P. 2003. "Assimilation Across Latino Generations." *American Economic Review* 93(2): 315–19.

Smith, James P. 2006. "Immigrants and Their Schooling." *Journal of Labor Economics* 24: 203–33.

Stanton-Salazar, Ricardo D. 2001. *Manufacturing Hope and Despair: The School and Kin Support Networks of U.S.-Mexican American Youth*. New York: Teachers College Press.

Stanton-Salazar, Ricardo D., and Sanford M. Dornbusch. 1995. "Social Capital and the Reproduction of Inequality: Information Networks among Mexican-Origin High School Students." *Sociology of Education* 68: 116–35.

Starr, Paul D. 1981. "Troubled Waters: Vietnamese Fisherfolk on America's Gulf Coast." *International Migration Review* 15: 226–38.

Steinberg, Stephen. 1981 *The Ethnic Myth: Race, Ethnicity, and Class in America*. Boston: Beacon Press.

Steinberg, Stephen. 1986. "The Rise of the Jewish Professional: Case Studies of Intergenerational Mobility." *Ethnic and Racial Studies* 9: 502–13.

Suárez-Orozco, Carola, and Marcelo Suárez-Orozco. 2007. "Education." Pp. 243–57 in *The New Americans: A Guide to Immigration since 1965*, edited by Mary C. Waters and Reed Ueda with Helen B. Marrow. Cambridge: Harvard University Press.

Suárez-Orozco, Marcelo. 1987. "Toward a Psychosocial Understanding of Hispanic Adaptation to American Schooling." Pp. 156–68 in *Success or Failure? Learning and the Languages of Minority Students*, edited by H.T. Trueba. New York: Newbury House.

Sue, Stanley, and Sumie Okazaki. 1990. "Asian American Educational Achievements: A Phenomenon in Search of an Explanation." *American Psychologist* 45: 913–20.

Swidler, Ann. 1986. "Culture in Action: Symbols and Strategies." *American Sociological Review* 51: 273–86.

Thieblot, A.J. 2002. "Technology and Labor Relations in the Construction Industry." *Journal of Labor Research* 23: 559–73.

Tilly, Charles. 1978. *From Mobilization to Revolution*. Reading: Addison-Wesley.

Tilly, Charles. 1990. "Transplanted Networks." Pp. 79–95 in *Immigration Reconsidered: History, Sociology, and Politics*, edited by Virginia Yans-McLaughlin. New York: Oxford University Press.

References

Tilly, Charles. 1998. *Durable Inequality*. Berkeley: University of California Press.

Tilly, Charles. 2005. *Identities, Boundaries, and Social Ties*. Boulder: Paradigm.

Times-Picayune. 1975 (Aug. 27). "Viets to Be Florida Fishermen." Section 2, p. 4.

Tyner, James A. 2007. "Filipinos: The Invisible Ethnic Community." Pp. 251–70 in *Contemporary Ethnic Geographies in America*, edited by Ines M. Miyares and Christopher Airriess. New York: Rowman & Littlefield.

Ueda, Reed. 2007. "Immigration in Global Historical Perspective." Pp. 14–28 in *The New Americans: A Guide to Immigration since 1965*, edited by Mary C. Waters and Reed Ueda with Helen B. Marrow. Cambridge: Harvard University Press.

United States Census Bureau. 2011. *Survey of Business Owners: Asian-Owned Businesses, 2007*. Washington, D.C.: U.S. Government Printing Office.

United States Department of Education. 2007. *Status and Trends in the Education of Racial and Ethnic Minorities*. Washington, D.C.: U.S. Department of Education, National Center for Education Statistics.

United States Department of Education. 2010. *Status and Trends in the Education of Racial and Ethnic Minorities*. Washington, D.C.: U.S. Department of Education, National Center for Education Statistics.

United States Department of Health and Human Services. 1993. "Report of the Office of Refugee Resettlement." *Migration World* 21: 24–5.

United States Department of Homeland Security. 2006. *Yearbook of Immigration Statistics, 2005*. Washington, D.C.: U.S. Department of Homeland Security, Office of Immigration Statistics.

United States Department of Homeland Security. 2012. *Yearbook of Immigration Statistics, 2011*. Washington, D.C.: U.S. Department of Homeland Security, Office of Immigration Statistics.

United States Department of Justice, Immigration and Naturalization Service. 2000. *1998 Statistical Yearbook of the Immigration and Naturalization Service*. Washington, D.C.: U.S. Government Printing Office.

Valenzuela, Angela, and Sanford M. Dornbusch. 1994. "Familism and Social Capital in the Academic Achievement of Mexican Origin and Anglo Adolescents." *Social Science Quarterly* 75: 18–36.

Villar, Maria de Lourdes. 1992. "Changes in Employment Networks among Mexican Immigrants in Chicago." *Urban Anthropology* 21: 385–97.

Vo, Linda Trinh, and Mary Yu Danico. 2004. "The Formation of Post-Suburban Communities: Koreatown and Little Saigon, Orange County." *International Journal of Sociology and Social Policy* 24: 15–45.

Vu, Lung, Mark Vanlandingham, Mai Do, and Carl L. Bankston III. 2009. "Evacuation and Return of Vietnamese New Orleanians Affected by Hurricane Katrina." *Organization and Environment* 22: 422–36.

Waldinger, Roger. 1994. "The Making of an Immigrant Niche." *International Migration Review* 28: 3–30.

Waldinger, Roger, and Cynthia Feliciano. 2004. "Will the New Second Generation Experience 'Downward Assimilation'? Segmented Assimilation Re-Assessed." *Ethnic and Racial Studies* 27: 376–402.

Warner, R. Stephen. 1994. "The Place of the Congregation in the American Religious Configuration." Pp. 54–99 in *American Congregations, Vol. 2*, edited by James P. Wind and James W. Lewis. Chicago: University of Chicago Press.

Weil, Frederick, Matthew R. Lee, and Edward S. Shihadeh. 2012. "The Burdens of Social Capital: How Socially-Involved People Dealt with Stress after Hurricane Katrina." *Social Science Research* 41: 110–19.

Wellman, Barry. 1999. *Networks in the Global Village: Life in Contemporary Communities*. Boulder: Westview Press.

Wierzbicki, Susan. 2004. *Beyond the Immigrant Enclave: Network Change and Assimilation*. New York: LFB Scholarly.

Williams, Raymond B. 1988. *Religion of Immigrants from India and Pakistan: New Threads in the American Tapestry*. New York: Cambridge University Press.

Wolf, Diane L. 1997. "Family Secrets: Transnational Struggles among Children of Filipino Immigrants." *Sociological Perspectives* 40: 457–82.

Wortham, Stanton, Katherine Mortimer, and Elaine Allard. 2009. "Mexicans as Model Minorities in the New Latino Diaspora." *Anthropology and Education Quarterly* 40: 388–404.

Yoo, Jeong Ah, and Allison Zipay. 2012. "Social Networks among Low Income Elderly Korean Immigrants in the United States." *Journal of Aging Studies* 26: 368–76.

Yoo, Jin-Kyung. 2000. "Utilization of Social Networks for Immigrant Entrepreneurship: A Case Study of Korean Immigrants in the Atlanta Area." *International Review of Sociology* 10: 347–63.

Yoon, In-Jin. 1995. "The Growth of Korean Entrepreneurship in Chicago." *Ethnic and Racial Studies* 18: 315–25.

Yoon, In-Jin. 2012. "Migration and the Korean Diaspora: A Comparative Description of Five Cases." *Journal of Ethnic and Migration Studies* 38: 413–35.

Young, Kim Dae. 1996. "The Limits of Ethnic Solidarity: Mexican and Ecuadorian Employment in Korean-Owned Businesses in New York City." Unpublished paper presented at the annual meetings of the American Sociological Association, New York City.

Zhan, Min, Stephen G. Anderson, and Saijun Zhang. 2012. "Utilization of Formal and Informal Financial Services among Immigrants in the United States." *Social Development Issues* 34(3): 1–17.

Zhou, Min. 1992. *Chinatown: The Socioeconomic Potential of an Urban Enclave*. Philadelphia: Temple University Press.

Zhou, Min. 1997. "Growing Up American: The Challenge Confronting

Immigrant Children and Children of Immigrants." *Annual Review of Sociology* 23: 63–95.

Zhou, Min. 2009. "How Neighborhoods Matter for Immigrant Children: The Formation of Educational Resources in Chinatown, Koreatown, and Pico Union, Los Angeles." *Journal of Ethnic and Migration Studies* 35: 1153–79.

Zhou, Min, and Carl L. Bankston III. 1992. "Variations in Economic Adaptation: The Case of Post-1965 Chinese, Korean, and Vietnamese Immigrants." *National Journal of Sociology* 6: 105–40.

Zhou, Min, and Carl L. Bankston III. 1994. "Social Capital and the Adaptation of the Second Generation: The Case of Vietnamese Youth in New Orleans." *International Migration Review* 28: 821–45.

Zhou, Min, and Carl L. Bankston III. 1998. *Growing Up American: How Vietnamese Children Adapt to Life in the United States.* New York: Russell Sage Foundation.

Zhou, Min, and Carl L. Bankston III. 2000. *Straddling Two Social Worlds: The Experience of Vietnamese Refugee Children in the United States.* New York: ERIC Clearinghouse on Urban Education.

Zhou, Min, and Carl L. Bankston III. 2001. "Family Pressure and the Educational Experience of the Daughters of Vietnamese Refugees." *International Migration* 39: 133–51.

Zhou, Min, and Carl L. Bankston III. 2006. "Delinquency and Acculturation in the Twenty-First Century: A Decade's Change in a Vietnamese American Community." Pp. 117–39 in *Immigration and Crime: Race, Ethnicity, and Violence*, edited by Ramiro Martinez, Jr. and Abel Valenzuela, Jr. New York: New York University Press.

Zhou, Min, and John Logan. 1989. "Returns on Human Capital in Ethnic Enclaves." *American Sociological Review* 54: 809–20.

Zhou, Min, Carl L. Bankston III, and Rebecca Kim. 2001. "Rebuilding Spiritual Lives in the New Land: Religious Practices among Southeast Asian Refugees in the United States." Pp. 37–70 in *Asian Immigration and Transplanting and Transforming Religions*, edited by Pyong Gap Min and Jung Ha Kim. Walnut Creek: Altamira Press.

Zontini, Elisabetta. 2010. "Enabling and Constraining Aspects of Social Capital in Migrant Families." *Ethnic and Racial Studies* 33: 816–31.

Index

Index

Index

Index